VOICES
BEYOND
BONDAGE

VOICES BEYOND BONDAGE

——————→ ←——————

AN ANTHOLOGY OF VERSE BY AFRICAN AMERICANS OF THE 19TH CENTURY

[signature] 4/28/15

EDITED BY ERIKA DESIMONE

AND FIDEL LOUIS

NEWSOUTH BOOKS
MONTGOMERY

NewSouth Books
105 S. Court Street
Montgomery, AL 36104

Library of Congress Cataloging-in-Publication Data

Voices Beyond Bondage : an Anthology of Verse by African Americans of the
19th Century / edited by Erika DeSimone and Fidel Louis.
pages cm
Includes index.

ISBN 978-1-58838-298-6 (hardcover) — ISBN 978-1-60306-276-3 (ebook)

1. American poetry—African American authors. 2. American poetry—19th
century. I. DeSimone, Erika, editor of compilation.
II. Louis, Fidel, editor of compilation.
PS508.N3V65 2014
811'.4080896073—dc23

2013042879

Design by Randall Williams

Printed in the United States of America
by Edwards Brothers Malloy

Contents

Introduction

ERIKA DESIMONE AND FIDEL LOUIS

Poetry universally is and always has been a source of inspiration, a means of education, and a conduit for culture and history. But for many 19th-century African Americans, poetry embodied something even more. In a society riddled by racial inequity, poetry became a safe haven through which African Americans preserved and shared their ideas, cultural knowledge, and heritage. By using the black-owned and other liberal media to publish their works, African Americans collectively created an ambitious literary movement which gave voice to the rich and multifaceted life of an oppressed people who were otherwise invisible to the larger society.

This anthology—the first to focus on African American writings as published in the early black-owned press—collects 150 poems published from 1827 to 1899. Whether these authors were slaves, former slaves, the children of slaves, or free people of African descent, all shared their writings in a way not possible before the 1827 birth of *Freedom's Journal* [see essay following this introduction]. We can also safely assume that each poem in *Voices Beyond Bondage* was penned not merely as an attempt to engage and inspire the hearts and minds of others but reflects a deliberate choice by its author to utilize the burgeoning black-owned media as a harbinger of change—making every poem in this book an act of subversion. As editors, we made our selections exclusively from 19th-century black-owned newspapers or pamphlets, and we took pains to ensure that—when authorship was traceable—each poem was written by an African American.

Nineteenth-century African Americans largely lived within marginalized communities or in the bonds of slavery; with rare exceptions in major cities, there was little intellectual and literary interaction between African Americans and the dominant Anglo American society. Yet despite marginalization, the authors included in this anthology were called to verse. They were not poets in the traditional or commercial sense, and most had no formal training in the craft of writing. They were not, to say the least, famous writers like Phillis Wheatley or Paul Lawrence Dunbar, nor icons like Frederick Douglass or Harriet Tubman. These were ordinary individuals who wrote poetry to share their experiences, emotions, and points of view with others.

The poems collected here were written during a particularly tumultuous time in American history—seven decades which encompassed slave revolts and abolitionism, the Civil War and the end of slavery, the short-lived hope of Reconstruction, and the grim despair of Jim Crow segregation. Rich in abundance and detail, this collection facilitates a more complex understanding of African American history—and American history as a whole—and provides insight into the literary, cultural, and political movements of these troubling years.

It is important to bear in mind a few things about the publications from which these poems have been collected. Whether they were regularly published like the *Weekly Anglo-African* or sporadically published like the *Louisville Newspaper*, editorially these newspapers were fiercely independent. Their writers and editors were often not professionally trained and the publications usually did not have deep-pocket backing. Profits (or losses) varied greatly and often mattered little to publishers whose ultimate goal was to provide a viable outlet for African Americans to express their voices and to impel social change.

Almost every black-owned newspaper of the period, no matter how small or sporadic, reserved a space for poetry, and from the hundreds and hundreds of poems we collected, we chose 150 for publication. Each poem provides a glimpse into the authors' daily lives, documenting their distinctive voices and individual interpretations of events. These narratives reveal realms of identity, shifting sentiments, and continuing struggles. Most importantly, each and every poem is evidence against the deep-seated stereotypes and institutionalized racism of the era, which portrayed African Americans as uneducated, illiterate, dependent on charity, stupid, lazy, and even subhuman—stereotypes which sadly linger today. In this regard, these poems stand sacred because they illustrate the fundamental humanity of an oppressed people.

One aspect of *Voices Beyond Bondage* that we celebrate most is the insight offered into the literacy of African Americans of the era. The stereotypes and popular histories portraying the "illiterate slave" or the "uneducable negro" are to some extent refuted simply by this book's existence. Our research supports the assertion that African American literacy was not as uncommon as history would have us believe, even among slaves. W. E. B. Du Bois estimated that by the end of the Civil War as many as 9 percent of slaves had achieved at least some degree of literacy; slavery historian Eugene Genovese suggested that Du Bois's estimate might have been quite low. Further, some slave owners, despite laws dating to the 1700s against slave education, did teach slaves to read so that they could study the Bible and be redeemed—in fact, some planters even set up "plantation schools" for slave children.

Among free African Americans, those called to God's service were among the best educated: literacy was vital to leading their congregations. Many of these churches spread literacy—openly or covertly—among both the free and the enslaved, creating unofficial learning centers under the guise of worship. Further, the Religious Society of Friends (Quakers) was not only an integral part of the Underground Railroad but also sponsored "colored schools" for both children and adults; these schools stretched from Canada to South Carolina and even into America's territories. In the years leading up to and following the Civil War, benevolent societies and the Freedmen's Bureau (among others) opened schools for people of color across the nation. From all this evidence, it is clear that literacy among African Americans was highly valued, and not especially rare; despite the enormous challenges of—and even threats inherent to—gaining a basic education, African Americans fervently sought learning. Can there be any doubt that the African American mind was a hungry mind, ravenous for intellectual stimulation?

Voices Beyond Bondage is one fruit of that hunger. Using poetry as an engine, the writers included in this book were among the pioneers of a literary movement which, in sum, was a catalyst for sweeping social change. Here is an innovative framework through which the rich literary life of African Americans can be analyzed. There are all kinds of poems in this anthology, with themes ranging from truest love to the worst dehumanization, from simple daily perseverance to civic outrage, from the silliest of humor to resolute strength gained from religion. Here we see the portrait of a people not merely engaged in their respective societies, but actively shaping them.

Most of the included poems had been lost to history, scattered among microfiche archives or hidden within bound volumes of various newspapers. Through egregious oversight, these publications have not been recognized for their true importance in American history, and therefore have long remained unexamined. The poems they contained fell by the wayside. Exhumed from source material, the poems in this book are a compilation of firsthand accounts in verse from ordinary people living— and thriving!—within marginalized circumstances.

Because of the breadth and sheer volume of this material we present these poems in five thematic sections, each beginning in the late 1820s and continuing chronologically throughout the century.

BONDAGE & CALLS FOR FREEDOM: While the title of this anthology promises to take readers on a journey "beyond bondage" and to delve deeper into the identities of 19th-century African Americans, we would be remiss if its first section did not address the bleakest stain on U.S. history—the race-based human chattel bondage system—and the voices that vehemently and bravely cried out for freedom. Until the end of the Civil War and the passage of the 13th amendment in 1865, slavery impacted politics, economics, criminal and civil law, human rights, and virtually every other aspect of society. Slaves themselves suffered the direct consequences of bondage, but even for African Americans who lived far from slaveholding states and territories, slavery loomed ever-present. No person of African descent in America was ever untouched by slavery—and the propaganda used to justify it—because race-based enslavement marked both free and enslaved African Americans as "other."

Through the 30 poems in "Bondage & Calls for Freedom," the monstrosity of slavery in America is laid bare. This section, a treasure trove of vivid personal voices, shows firsthand how deeply African Americans were affected by slavery. Some authors recounted a dismal time of sadness and whippings, others of fears and captivity, and others reflected upon the humiliation of being treated as livestock. Imagine the anger and disgust of the anonymous author who wrote "Farewell, freedom! farewell, pleasure!/I must back to slavery go;/Toil to swell a master's treasure,/Through a life of pain and woe./Palsied be the power which gave/Back the man to be the slave!"

As stirring as those words are, we are reminded repeatedly throughout this section of another atrocious facet of slavery. Poem after poem recounts how slave families were callously sundered: children torn from their mothers' breasts and sold, and husbands and wives forced apart at the auction block. When H. M. wrote "Poor doom'd one, hark! the hammer falls, the wretch asserts his right,/He tears her from her Boy, to whom she clings with all her might/'My child!' she screams—'In mercy buy my own, my darling boy/Quick! buy him quick! You cannot sure my life blood thus destroy." S/he was recounting no extraordinary scene—it was common practice to sell children away from their mothers. In expressing these scenes in verse, H. M. and others helped to create a literary movement essential to advancing their calls for freedom.

Despite the horrors recounted, the most striking message of this section is the vital sense of moral justice. These authors understood that fighting for justice and mobilizing their fellow brethren were not merely a matter of politics, but rather a vocational call. These writers were determined not to let America's racist institutions dictate their people's destiny.

DEDICATIONS & REMEMBRANCES spans a breadth of human emotions—emotions which many slaveholders contended that African Americans were fundamentally incapable of feeling—and covers a wide range of topics. The poems here are directly addressed or dedicated "to"—whether the addressee was a departed family member, an abolitionist, a scoundrel of a politician, or even a pen.

About half of the poems in this section are remembrances, written to mothers, children, sisters, and even ministers, and offers us a number of the most touching moments in this anthology. Death touches us all, but in the 19th century, before the advent of modern medicine, death came far more frequently and far earlier than most of us experience today. These authors found solace and comfort by writing memorials to those who had touched them most deeply in life. As these poems show, healing is never easy and mourning does not pass quickly. Whose heart would not break upon reading "Under the Snow," a parent's mournful farewell to a lost baby: "Under the Snow our baby lies,/The fringed lids dropped o'er her eyes;/The tiny hands upon her breast,/Like twin-born lilies taking rest."

Some poem topics in this section are highly politicized. Daniel Hayes was brave enough in "Southrons," a poem penned in response to the 1854 Kansas-Nebraska Act, to document the institutionalized rape of female slaves by masters and overseers in Southern states (i.e. Southrons) to promote slave "breeding." When Hayes recounts "[Slaves] Though born of slave mothers, begot by yourselves" we are reminded that the children born to these abused women were—by their own fathers!—either put to work as slaves or sold as property. Is it any wonder that "Southrons," from first line to last, drips with anger and revulsion? In another poem, "To Mr. Fillmore: On His Retirement from the Presidency," an author known only as "Q" brazenly calls President Fillmore—who was no friend of the abolitionist—stupid, fat, and unchristian. Q's poem is so vivid we can almost hear him exhaling with relief at the retirement of a president who "punish[es] men, by fine and jail,/Who keep the Golden Rule" and inhaling the hope of a better future. Authors like these, for whom the color of their skin was almost a crime and the law far from equal, are among the bravest in this anthology. Who knows what consequences publishing poems such as these could have wrought?

Two poems in this section express the very heart of this anthology as they directly celebrate literacy. In "My Pen," Frank Addison Mowig Philom exalts the knowledge that reading and writing afford him. "My pen, my pen,/my joy and my pride,/My idol I worship each day;/A gem which adversity giveth to me,/Shall speak of the shackles, the bond and the free." In "The Palladium of Liberty," a poem written to commemorate the inaugural issue of the Ohio-based newspaper by the same name, G. W. Roots takes celebration of literacy one step further and honors the power of the circulated word: "This paper has been presented to us/ By the colored people of Columbus/We hope to delineate the chains of slavery/By the force of Palladium of Liberty." As all of the poems in this anthology are culled from black-owned newspapers, Roots's poem is particularly poignant—the circulated word is a powerful word, ageless and inspiring.

IN MORAL & CIVIC PERSPECTIVES, the authors describe how paramount it was to lead upright lives and how morality informed their under-standing of civic duty. This section includes poems from all 72 years that this anthology encompasses. Yet despite spanning seven decades, a remarkable consistency of voice runs though this section. A far cry from the depictions of "shiftless negroes" in the mainstream media, these authors proudly tell us how deeply their convictions and morals ran, and how that morality became the backbone of African American communities.

Half the poems in the section celebrate hard work, perseverance, humbleness, and upright living. When the reader is admonished to "Set Yer Teeth an' Come Agin!," it is clear that we are reading the words of one who espouses no idleness or laziness: "Don't loaf around an' kick when luck/Don't seem to come your way, but buck/Agin adversity till you/Through breakin' clouds kin see the blue." This author modeled the roughness of his/her words to match the true resilience of his/her de-termination. J. C. O., of upstate New York, writes in a more traditional voice in "Fearless and Faithful," but there remains no doubt that we are reading the words of an author dedicated to the upright life: "Labor fear-less, labor faithful,/Labor while the day shall last,/For the shadows of the evening/Soon thy sky will overcast;/Ere shall end thy day of labor,/ Ere shall rest thy manhood's sun,/Strive with every power within thee,/

That the appointed task be done."

Other authors in "Moral & Civic Perspectives" share their morality more abstractly yet no less poignantly. In "The Black Beauty," the anonymous author asserts that she is beautiful, and beautiful to Jesus Christ her savior. She wrote this in 1827—more than 100 years before the "black is beautiful" mantra of civil rights and black power movements of the 1960s and '70s. She asserted her beauty at a time when African features and traits were often regarded as ugly and a mark of fundamental inferiority. Even more radical is this author's assertion that Jesus would love an African American woman not *despite* her race, but rather as *included* in God's whole and perfect creation; this idea would have bordered on blasphemy in many mainstream congregations of the day. But this brave author knew the courage of her convictions: "Black, indeed, appears my skin,/Beauteous, comely, all within:/Black, when by affliction press'd/Beauteous, when in Christ I rest."

Another example of morals informing civic perspective is S. H. Johnson's 1891 poem, "Which." Here Johnson calls on his African American brothers and sisters to be advocates for their own education. After the Civil War, many freed people, having been entirely dependent on their masters, lacked the basic skills with which to navigate society. This lacking, coupled with Jim Crow laws, put African Americans on a road to perpetual poverty and only reinforced the myth of white supremacy. Bearing witness to this cycle in the 20-plus years following the Civil War, Johnson must have recognized that education was one of the few weapons which could advance African Americans and begin to dissolve race-based inequity. Thus, the author asks "Will halls of learning always be/A 'factor' which we fail to see?/Will banks always to us be strange,/And commerce deemed beyond our range?" In so doing, he calls his people to a better life through education.

REMINISCENCE & HUMOR is comprised largely of poems about sweet longing sentiments and day-to-day happenings. While a minority of these poems (such as J. C. Holly's beautiful "Grief") do address more sober subjects, the section reminds us that the 19th century was not all drama and tumult. Here, we find authors particularly interested in telling us how they went through life in the most ordinary ways, making this section robust with quaint stories and delightful humor.

While momentous events may define an era or a movement, and births and deaths, marriages and windfalls may demarcate our lives, life itself is mostly lived in small moments during which relationships deepen, habits are forged, traditions become venerated. No poem presented here reminds us of this better than "Promise of the Past," an author's sweet pining for the days of his childhood: "'Tis but of fleeting years a score/ Since father used to call—/'My son, 'tis time you got to bed;/Come, say good night to all.'" "Promise of the Past" exemplifies a quiet agelessness that runs throughout this section; the sentiments expressed here are as relevant today as they were 150 years ago.

"Reminiscence & Humor" also offers us something hardly presented elsewhere in this anthology—humor. Laughing is a most basic human quality, and many of the authors in this section were intent on making us do just that. Lunsford Lane's "Misconstrued" blames poor pronunciation for a missed chance at romance; "Moveing Day" contends that the kerfuffle of moving is far more confusing than earthquakes or battalions in retreat; "Kindness to Animals" is a wonderfully silly nonsense poem; and in "Humidity" Louis Howard Latimer painfully laments the stickiness of a summer's day. Poems such as these offer us a little levity and, more importantly, remind us that laughter in itself is sometimes also resilience. Despite all the hardship, prejudice, and marginalization that 19th-century African Americans endured, they were not afraid to laugh—not afraid to inspire laughter and share it. In this regard, these "silly" poems are the human spirit.

SPIRIT & THE NATURAL WORLD closes the volume on a note of faith and humanism. The 33 poems on this subject confirm the eminence of God and attest the beauty and wonder of His creations in nature. The section's authors speak of how their faith inspired strength and hope, of how they found comfort in God's word, and of how they drew spiritual renewal from the beauty of the world around them.

The exclusively Christian themes within the section are not surprising given how seamlessly Christianity was woven into the fabric of 19th-century American society. Notwithstanding small minorities of followers of other faiths and the spiritual practices of Native Americans, the America of the 19th century was a Christian America: many laws and ordinances were written around Christian practice, and societal roles conformed to the Christian tradition. Regardless of denomination, faith in Christ informed everyday life in that era.

Every section of this anthology echoes of Christianity in some way, whether in cries against the injustices of slavery, remembrances of the departed, criticisms of politicians, attestations of morals, or solace in hope. For African Americans in particular, the Christian church was more than just a place of worship. Churches served as centers of education, stops on the Underground Railroad, pulpits for abolitionists and teetotalers, and spaces where African American perspectives on Christianity could be explored and methods of worship hewed to their communities' needs.

It is from this perspective that "Spirit & the Natural World" must be read. These are not only poems of faith and wonderment, but rather an extension of this basic worldview. Poems describing the beauty and bounty of nature are also poems of thanksgiving and/or praise. In some poems, such as Mrs. E. Coutee's eloquent, soft-spoken "Forest Prayer," the natural and the spiritual worlds are intrinsically intertwined: "Before the balmy breath of morn/The echo gives from hunter's horn,/Then soft and still as is His will,/The loving God goes through the wood." Other poems such as Elizabeth M. Sargent's "Great Deeds" do not reference God directly, but rather express a subtler spiritual undertone: "Gently and stilly/Falleth the dew—/It jars not the lily/Hiding from view;/The lily, from the heavens fed, offereth her prayer,/And silently the incense riseth on the air!" For these authors, God—whether in the form of God the creator, Jesus the son, or the Holy Spirit—was not just in the churches so central to their communities, but imbued throughout everyday life. Their words sing proudly of their faith in the Lord God, evidencing that African American traditions of Christian worship were just as strong, and perhaps in some respects stronger, as Anglo-based interpretations. Although this is the subtlest subversion presented in this anthology, it is subversive nonetheless.

One notable exception to this Christian-centric writing is George M. Horton's "On the Evening and Morning." Here Horton frames his poem around classical influences, recalling the ancient gods of Rome and Greece. However, it is clear from the poem's context that the pagan gods referenced are not held as God, but rather as the stuff of myth.

We present "Spirit & the Natural Word" as the closing section of this book not because these poems are least in importance or poetic merit—in fact, some of the poems in this section are among the most beautiful in the book. On the contrary, we end *Voices Beyond Bondage* with this section because of its uplifting messages of faith, resilience, and humanity.

· · · · · · · ·

RESEARCH FOR *Voices Beyond Bondage* began 19 years ago when Fidel Louis was working on his master's thesis on the history of the black press in America. It was then that he began gathering poems from 19th century black-owned newspapers; Erika DeSimone joined him in this work in 2002. Since then we have amassed a collection of nearly 1,000 poems—most taken from microfilm at public libraries, although in more recent years the Internet made this research eminently easier. This anthology has been a labor of love—created and shaped without access to university libraries, backing from research grants, or the help of research assistants. After identifying those poems which met our criteria for this anthology, we chose 150 of the most compelling and passionate to preserve and share in this volume. We hope that you enjoy reading these poems as much as we enjoy presenting them to you.

FOUR PIONEERING PUBLISHERS OF THE NINETEENTH CENTURY

· · ·

Clockwise from top left: Samuel Cornish; David Ruggles;
Frederick Douglass; and T. Thomas Fortune.

The Early Black-Owned Press and the Poetry Movement: A Journalistic Perspective

Erika DeSimone and Fidel Louis

I n 1761, Jupiter Hammon, a slave from Long Island with undeni-
able writing talent, became the first African American to have his
poems published in what would soon become the United States of
America. Twelve years later, Phillis Wheatley, a slave in Boston, became
the first African American woman to have her writings published in
colonial America. These two African Americans possessed such enor-
mous literary talents as to attract the attention of the mainstream media.
Thus, the foundation of the African American poetry tradition was laid.
But without the cooperation of the Anglo-run mainstream media (and
without permission from their owners), these two founders of the African
American literary tradition would never have been published, and their
voices would have faded into the ether.

Perhaps history would have recorded dozens of other early African
American writers, but few newspapers or journals in the eighteenth and
early nineteenth centuries bothered to publish African American writers
or even include articles of interest to black communities—despite the
fact that the African American population was steadily growing. Thus,
"publication" for African Americans in the colonial and postcolonial
periods largely meant distributing two-page handwritten pamphlets or
encoding messages and "news" into hand-sewn quilts. However, by the
early decades of the 19th century, as more African Americans attained
freedom and/or education, the need for black communities to have their
own newspapers became increasingly pressing. Unless African Americans
had their own vehicle of communication, how could they ever combat
the mainstream media's libelous, racist misrepresentations and mischar-

acterizations? How could they examine issues of the day from their own perspectives? How could they link their communities, advertise their goods and services, share information, or empower their voices? How could African American writers have their poems and stories published without their own journals?

That was exactly what Peter Williams Jr. of New York, an Episcopal priest, was asking. He was passionate about creating a media outlet for that would be completely under African American ownership and editorial control. He knew that in 1822 the Manumission Society in Ohio had started a newspaper devoted to the cause of African Americans (*Independent Press & Freedom's Advocate*) but that, in his view, was a drop in the bucket. As an influential ordained priest and educator at the African Free School in New York City, Williams's list of friends and associates was huge. He worked out a plan, put the finances together, and convinced Samuel E. Cornish and John B. Russwurm to join him in launching a weekly newspaper. These three clergymen knew they were making history, and Cornish in particular worked tirelessly to solicit, write, and edit articles for the first issue. Their paper would be the first step in rewriting the "rules" of American media.

On March 14, 1827, African Americans in New York had the opportunity to read *Freedom's Journal*, the first black-owned and operated newspaper in the nation. Circulation was rather small (about 3,000 copies), but that premiere issue was read by almost every literate African American in New York and was praised by the liberal and abolitionist media. The format was well-presented, the news articles and editorials were finely written, and the paper was free from the usual clutter of socially demeaning ads. The liberal press saw in *Freedom's Journal* the emergence of a new kind of news reporting and praised Cornish for his writings. Except for the *New York Observer* with its plentiful racist remarks, the local media received *Freedom's Journal* with fanfare. But the best was yet to come. Even though the *Journal*'s layout was a mere four pages, Cornish dedicated a permanent space for an open call poetry column, thereby offering ordinary African Americans both a creative outlet and an impetus to engage in the act of writing. The column proved immensely popular among readers and was a key factor in the newspaper's overall success.

For the next two years, *Freedom's Journal* was the sole voice of the African American community in New York and a solid forum for a quickly growing poetry movement. It allowed a North Carolinian slave named George M. Horton, one of the finest wordsmiths in this anthology, to sharply highlight how bondage ravaged the lives of the enslaved, and granted a superbly talented young writer using the name "Africus" the opportunity to illustrate how slavery was a crime against humanity. Cornish, who discovered the talent of these and many other authors, was now at the center of a literary movement and a cultural shift. Not only could his influence be felt in many authors' writings, but he also encouraged his readers to submit letters challenging his editorial opinion, making *Freedom's Journal* truly the voice of its readership. *Freedom's Journal* thus gave undeniable proof against the then too-prevalent idea that African Americans were inherently stupid, illiterate, or incapable of participating in "civilized" society.

The paper, though not profitable, got better over time. Cornish, who was not trying to impress the establishment or win over advertisers, focused his attention on the delicate balance of printing an outstanding paper while making his publication attractive to a community with a high rate of illiteracy. Tackling that double whammy was no easy task, but Cornish was praised for his tenacity and for educating African Americans through his activism. He also, in both articles and speeches, urged African Americans to read and share the profound works of Jupiter Hammon and Phillis Wheatley as well as other nascent authors of color. As a college graduate and a clergyman who had for many years written for abolitionist papers, Cornish was more qualified than most to speak authoritatively on literary matters. His ideas were novel, but even those who tried to paint him as elitist agreed that his journalistic integrity commanded respect. He often said he found solace in the poetry movement because it was an accessible, not overly inflammatory niche. He would print poems by Anglo American authors if the works' underlying themes related to "uplift[ing] the colored race," as he would say. (In fact, almost all the black-owned newspapers to follow would take Cornish's cue; it became common practice to run poems of liberal and abolitionist Anglo American authors.) Through his example and dedication, Cornish nurtured many talented writers of poetry.

HOWEVER, CORNISH SOON BECAME disenchanted with his comrades. Certainly Cornish's concerns were grave. Co-editor John Russwurm, who had by now become deeply involved in what aspired to be an international abolitionist coalition, made an effort to own *Freedom's Journal* outright, with the idea that he would turn the paper profitable. In fact, Russwurm did gain control of the paper for a time but failed to prove his leadership. The tensions between the two men led Cornish to resign despite the pleas of Peter Williams. Among other things, Cornish's departure was a blow for poets and their growing voice. *Freedom's Journal* continued for a few months without Cornish, but ultimately closed its doors in 1829.

What Cornish did next caught everyone by surprise. That same year, he returned with a stable of writers and started the *Rights of All*, a paper that was widely sought after by poets. His supporters hoped this paper would replace the *Freedom's Journal* in terms of political direction, editorial content, and cultural responsibility. And it did just that: Cornish ensured that the fine writings, touching stories, and open literary debates were back in full gear. The *Rights of All* was indisputably Cornish's paper. In a permanent space next to his editorial column, Cornish emphasized the differences between the *Rights of All* and *Freedom's Journal*, especially with regard to the literary movement. After all, Cornish, as the most ardent supporter of the literary movement, was also keenly aware of the risk of neglecting it. The *Rights of All* was wildly successful, so much so that women's rights advocate Mary Gordon, along with Mrs. M. Christain, a wealthy Bostonian alumni of the Abiel Smith School, and other notables regularly contributed their talents to the paper. They wrote movingly about what they and their ancestors had gone through—no freedom in the land of the free, no equality in a country founded on all men being created equal. Although the paper lasted only a year, it was considered the quintessence of the poetry movement and a significant achievement in Cornish's journalistic career.

As word spread that African Americans were reading more than ever, efforts to create and circulate new newspapers began mounting. Freedom of speech was the drumbeat. John G. Stewart, an ambitious young entrepreneur, started the *African Sentinel and Journal of Liberty* in 1831 on the premise that he would continue Cornish's legacy, but his paper, which covered too many political issues, had no true sense of editorial direction. Published sporadically, the *African Sentinel* was mocked as being a pamphlet in large format, and it did not contribute to the poetry movement. When it soon became obvious that his dream of having a weekly paper could not be sustained, Stewart shut down the *African Sentinel.*

For a while, it looked as though Cornish's efforts could not be duplicated. Financing a black-owned, independent newspaper was tough. Mainstream newspapers were kept afloat by large advertising revenues from local merchants or by cash infusions from government agencies, but black-owned newspapers had almost no such support and relied heavily on their subscribers for revenue. And it was a constant fight to get subscribers to pay their fees—newspaper subscriptions were "luxury" items in most African American communities. Case in point: the *Anti-Slavery Advocate*, a pamphlet started in 1834, struggled to become a full-fledged newspaper; ultimately, the paper was not financially viable. Though short-lived, the *Anti-Slavery Advocate* did achieve success in one respect: the paper gave voice to a new breed of writers such as Martin R. Delany, Philip Bell, and Thomas Hamilton, all of whom would later offer their talents to other black-owned newspapers.

Cornish was too passionate and driven to remain out of the game for long. To keep the black-owned press alive and active, he joined forces with Phillip Bell in early 1837 and began the *Weekly Advocate,* which they renamed six months later to the *Colored American.* Once again, writers of poetry had their own column and a space for their voices. Cornish's unflinching determination further fueled the poetry movement and his methods achieved fairly great results, despite the fact that the editors were not always in harmony: Bell, a brilliant journalist, was more argumentative and left-leaning than Cornish. The *Colored American* ran for two years, supported largely by Cornish's loyal readership. The closing of the paper again left a void in the world of the black-owned presses.

Into this journalistic maelstrom stepped David Ruggles. Ruggles, a seasoned journalist, realized that he could slash operating costs by owning a press, thus cutting out external print shops. He began the *Mirror of Liberty* in 1838. Having written for William Lloyd Garrison's well-established abolitionist paper the *Liberator*, Ruggles's design was to create as broad a readership as possible—and he was willing to take big risks achieve just that. He took a radical step, advocating strong alliances between the abolitionist and women's rights movements. As a black-owned newspaper that uniquely spoke to both Anglo and African American communities, the *Mirror of Liberty* was the most provocative black-owned paper to date. Ruggles published both African American women and Anglo American abolitionist women, including the famous poet Lydia M. Child. Louise Smith, who would later edit the *Liberty Star*—making her one of the first female African American editors in the country—started her writing career with Ruggles. *Mirror of Liberty* quickly became known as an all-out fighter for social justice and equality and as a safe haven for poets and political writers, many of whom had no opportunity to publish their radical liberal views elsewhere.

A black-owned newspaper that was home to both African- and Anglo American causes was unheard of, but Ruggles was shrewd. He published the paper in New York City but also circulated it in Hartford and Boston where those living in African American enclaves had begun integrating into society at large. Ruggles believed that African Americans who integrated themselves into mainstream society should have their "achievement" celebrated and should be set as examples. This was a radical notion and might have sunk the paper entirely, but his message resonated with the emerging class of educated African Americans. Ruggles furiously wrote about the lack of that group's representation in both the black-owned and mainstream media, offering an outlet to an otherwise neglected subset of the populace.

However, African American nationalists from the South and cynics from Anglo-owned abolitionist papers vilified Ruggles's radical views, temporarily overshadowing his reputation. He closed the paper; his printing shop went out of business; and poor health slowed down his activism in the Underground Railroad. The press repeatedly observed that the closing of the *Mirror of Liberty* was a major setback to the black-owned press and the growing poetry movement. But Ruggles would not go away, particularly because the literary movement—that had become his soul—was now at a crossroads. Instead of disappearing, Ruggles did what only he had the know-how and audacity to pull off: in 1834, he opened the nation's first true African American bookstore. Located at 67 Lispenard Street in New York City, Ruggles's bookstore served as both a store and reading room dedicated to African American interests. Customers could buy or read weekly papers, periodicals, and, of course, books. Copies of the *Northern Star and Freeman's Advocate* were sold alongside stacks of local pamphlets and religious papers—all of which sold fast. Authors were invited to promote their books, and poets were welcome to read their verses. Ruggles effectively transformed his bookstore into a cultural learning center. Some nights, so he said, Ruggles had to physically remove materials-delinquent Martin Delany from the reading room or yell at the *Liberator's* William C. Nell, who had taken up an "unofficial residence." When his mentor and former boss William Lloyd Garrison visited, Ruggles tried to preempt potential conflict by denying access to incendiary minister Henry Highland Garnet and the oft-quarrelsome *Colored American* editor Philip Bell. Learning breathed in everything; intellectual debates flared up; the energy of the literary movement exploded. The influence of Ruggles's cultural center was felt in everything from educators' almost insurmountable tasks and clergymen's efforts against illiteracy to the expansion of the poetry movement itself. In 1845, the Census Bureau published the jaw-dropping fact that 57.1 percent of the African American population in New York could read—the highest rate of literacy to date. Encouraging news!

However, slavery in the South and in western territories remained a great barrier to African Americans' intellectual growth and a huge threat to the black-owned newspaper enterprise. To address that issue and to support the education of their brethren, David Jenkins and a group of friends in Columbus, Ohio, began the short-lived *Palladium of Liberty* in 1843. Getting it on track was hard and maintaining distribution from Columbus was unfortunately even harder. Still, the paper was seen as a symbolic continuation of the Manumission Society's *Freedom's Advocate*. Jenkins's ardent supporters believed the paper failed to gain national recognition because of racism inherent in the mainstream media distribution channels, while his bickering rivals claimed that the paper failed because it was not professionally edited and did not have a strong enough attachment to the poetry movement. These issues and others forced the closing of the *Palladium of Liberty* a year later.

AT THIS POINT, THE poetry movement's progress was patchy. Despite its previous success, there was a continuing assumption that the poetry tradition was difficult to expand. Challenges for the black-owned newspapers were also immense. Ruggles, having struggled to win support, decided he would have to take this journalistic cultural phenomenon to a larger scale. To him, the interconnectedness of southern and northern African Americans was amiss. For example, the unity that Peter Williams Jr. had begun preaching was yet to materialize nationally and the universal education for emancipated slaves that John Teasman had envisioned was yet to reach the ears of many in the South. Ruggles concluded that it would take a newspaper with an exceptionally strong voice to effect change on such a wide range of issues. Once again, Ruggles ducked. Working covertly, Ruggles convinced his old-time buddy, who was then lecturing in the British Isles to escape his owner, to come back to New York. Ruggles helped settle his friend's manumission fees and then, after a time, passed him the torch. This friend was none other than Frederick Douglass, and his work would alter the course of American history.

When he first returned to New York, Douglass—in addition to lending his stunning oratory gifts to various antislavery groups—worked as a contributor to both the *Ram's Horn* and the highly influential *National Anti Slavery Standard*. But Ruggles steered Douglass towards full-time journalism, encouraging Douglass to begin his own antislavery weekly. Douglas was initially reluctant but ultimately agreed to Ruggles's proposal.

On December 3, 1847, the *North Star* circulated its first issue. The paper was an instant success among New York's and Boston's African American populations and soon reached readers as far away as Virginia and North Carolina. Its editorial board was comprised of three intellectual heavyweights: outspoken-yet-eloquent Frederick Douglass, shrewd Martin Delany, and clever and politically active William C. Nell. They established the *North Star* "under the complete control and direction of the victims of slavery and oppression and its influence would be felt for years to come."

Through the quality of its material, the scope of its circulation, and its bold editorial stance, the *North Star* became the first paper strong enough to depose the societal myth that African Americans were a race of "invisible" beings. For as Douglass wrote in the *North Star's* inaugural issue, "The man who has suffered the wrong is the man to demand redress." The *North Star* became the thrilling voice of the oppressed, a call to arms that energized thousands, and the medium for African Americans' views on all manner of topics. The paper quickly became a potential threat to both the established media and pro-slavery advocates and served as the lifeblood for African American poets. From here on out, African Americans could no longer be pushed to the edges of society or dismissed as chattle; the *North Star* thrust African Americans' plights and passions onto the national stage as no other black-owned newspaper had.

Douglass couldn't have been more joyful. Regarded by many as a prominent scholar and bon vivant, he urged pro-reform poets to present every aspect of their lives in great detail as protest against the terrible social climate and living conditions African Americans faced. Following in Cornish's tradition, Douglass insisted that every issue contain a poetry column. Douglass's dedication to the poetry movement meant that the *North Star* (and later *Frederick Douglass' Paper*) soon became a mainstay for Frances Ellen Watkins [Harper]'s works and James M. Whitfield's literary cradle. The readership's overwhelming response to *North Star's* open call for poetry meant that the paper often received more poems that it could print.

For four consecutive years, the *North Star* was the darling of the black-owned newspapers, offering many writers and political activists a "home base" through which they could express their views. In the *North Star*, Douglass had created a wide-reaching space for open dialogue and discussions of relevant issues from an African American perspective, although some contributors—especially fugitive slaves or those still in bondage—chose to use aliases or to remain anonymous to protect themselves.

Of all the editors of the era, only Douglass pursued the poetry tradition through a nationalistic perspective and connected it with current politics. As long as the victimized and the downtrodden continued to speak out, Douglass would find them an outlet. That was evident in 1851 when he merged the *North Star* with Gerrit Smith's *Liberty Party Paper* to form the even more radical *Frederick Douglass' Paper* as part of his response to his competition. He lashed out at detractors of the "political enterprise," had legitimate beefs with other editorial writers, and motivated African Americans into becoming more politically involved and astute. *Frederick Douglass' Paper* proved to be even more successful than the *North Star* and ran uninterrupted until 1860, making it the longest-running and most influential black-owned newspaper to date.

Douglass's approach, however well-intentioned and successful, drew a backlash. The religious conservative wing retaliated against his radicalism. In 1854, the African Methodist Episcopal Church published the *Christian Recorder*—a four-page weekly—for "the dissemination of Religion, Morality, Literature and Science." But rather than focusing on religion and morality, editor John P. Campbell tended to the macabre and put much emphasis on human tragedies. However, although he filled his paper with scores of stories about suffering, Campbell also made room for poetry—although most of the poems he published recounted hardship. Because of Campbell's unpopular editorial focus, the first incarnation of the paper didn't last long. However, when Elisha Weaver resurrected the *Recorder* in 1861, the paper became more attractive, becoming one of the strongest journalistic voices for more religious/conservative African Americans, offering its readership a solid outlet for wholesome and devotional poetry. The paper became so popular that the *Recorder* is still published today (though publication has not been continuous).

Also during 1854, the *Weekly Anglo-African* emerged as a roaring lion and a new outlet for poets. This paper had a strong positive campaign and set the stage for a reevaluation of family values—an axis upon which African Americans could potentially reclaim their cultural identities. Editor Thomas Hamilton, who was known to respectfully criticize Douglass's works and tip his hat to Ruggles, generated an explosion of ideas among his readers and offered the first real competition to *Frederick Douglass' Paper*. The *Weekly Anglo-African* had six zealous contributing editors ready to do anything to serve the core of their constituency and within a few months became a veritable repository of African American poetry. The paper marketed itself as a progressive, less elitist publication than *Frederick Douglass' Paper*, reaching out to the large population of African Americans whose primary focus was not intellectual debate and academic argument but who still needed and deserved an African American perspective on everyday news and happenings.

Other papers such as the *Mirror of the Times* grew to claim their slice of the pie. By now, black-owned newspapers had carved a firm niche in the media, and the growing competition forced Douglass to reconsider his approach to journalism. In 1859, Douglass began printing *Douglass' Monthly* as a supplement to *Frederick Douglass' Paper*, and the following year closed *Frederick Douglass' Paper* entirely. *Douglass' Monthly* continued but by 1863 the Civil War had taken its toll on Douglass's efforts and he shut the paper down.

Unfortunately, the Civil War brought black-owned newspapers to a near standstill. Distribution channels were regularly interrupted and intercepted. Offices shut down as the war became more intense. Many of the movement's pioneers traded newspaper work for political appointments. Other leaders such as Highland Garnet (who had become a contributing editor to the *Weekly Anglo-African* before the war) quietly faded into the background. While the *Weekly Anglo-African*, along with a few other papers, ultimately survived the war (and had managed to keep the poetry movement alive), all the black-owned papers were severely crippled.

The glaring need for a strong black-owned paper to fill the gap left a window of opportunity for an editor to fill Douglass's shoes. Dr. Louis

Charles Roudanez didn't wait for the war to end to grasp that opportunity. In 1864, he founded the *New Orleans Tribune*, the first major black-owned newspaper to be published in both English and French editions. Dr. Roudanez, an advocate for social justice, recognized that the South was becoming more cosmopolitan and tested his market by printing three issues a week for the first three months. Not only was the *Tribune* well-received among African Americans, it was also praised by Southern white intellectuals. Dr. Roudanez aimed to make his paper an intellectual forum and devoted as much space as possible to that end, including a column for poetry. The *Tribune* effectively took the leadership among black-owned newspapers, and in the space of three months it became highly influential—especially within the poetry movement. Then Dr. Roudanez, after mulling over the idea and discussing it with his editorial staff, turned a new corner in the annals of African American history: in October 1864, he began to publish the *Tribune* daily. A daily paper dedicated to African American needs was a truly innovative step, making the *Tribune* even more popular.

After the war ended in 1865 and slaves were proclaimed free, more black-owned newspapers and journals popped up. Southerners began to compete in earnest with Northerners for a broader readership. However, the Reconstruction era was so devastating and politicized that besides the *Tribune* the only Southern post-war papers to last two years or more were the *Colored Tennessean* by William Scott and the *Loyal Georgian*. However, even these short-lived papers played an important role in preserving and reinvigorating what was by now not just a literary movement, but an honored tradition. For example, the *Freeman's Press* and the *Black Republican* both focused largely on printing verses written by newly freed slaves.

In the years immediately after the war, Dr. Roudanez was possibly the most influential African American in the nation. His opinion on social issues was highly regarded, and he was praised for his leadership of the *Tribune*. Even though Reconstruction was tumultuous, he managed to keep the *Tribune* in production until April 1868. In 1869, he resurrected the paper for another year, but it ceased publication permanently in 1870.

In 1873, after three years without a large-circulation black-owned paper, David Young launched the *Concordia Eagle* from a small Louisiana town on the Mississippi border. For the next seventeen years, the *Eagle* was widely read and highly respected. Its geographic base afforded it a wide circulation that reached large concentrations of African Americans as far away as Maryland and North Carolina, helping to create a readership monopoly among Southern freed people. With its open verbal battle against the status quo and its strong attachment to the poetry tradition (its dedicated space for poetry was the first column of the front page), the *Eagle* reflected a new post-war tone. Contributors and poets were proud to talk about those who helped African Americans rebuild after the war; they praised former abolitionists who were now founding schools for African American children and offering financial support to benevolent societies; they revered the likes of Abraham Lincoln and General N. P. Banks; and they encouraged African Americans to pursue education and celebrate their freedom. As millions of freed slaves began building new lives, this re-politicizing of the poetry movement jump-started African American literature as a whole. The success of the *Eagle* prompted the editors from smaller papers such as the *Georgetown Planet* and the *American Citizen* to copy Young's style. These papers never quite captured Young's essence, but many enjoyed modest success as the numbers of literate African Americans grew and readers preferred having multiple papers to choose from.

In 1881 the *Concordia Eagle* found that it had a strong competitor—one that in fact posed a serious challenge to every black-owned publication. The *New York Globe*, a weekly paper edited by Timothy Thomas Fortune, made a triumphant entry into the market. The *Globe* offered fine articles and excellent reporting, and printed some of the most interesting writings on slavery and its aftermath. Despite the strength of the paper, the *Globe*'s downfall came when Fortune began using it to promote incendiary political ideas, accusing the Republican Party of abandoning African Americans after Reconstruction and calling for African Americans not to remain loyal to Republicans based solely on the emancipation. These views ultimately caused Fortune's backers to pull their support, and he closed the *Globe* in 1884.

Fortune was so opinionated and devoted to his career that he started another paper that same year—the *New York Freeman*. Despite insufficient funding, he managed to keep the *Freeman* afloat for more than three years—thanks in large measure to the training he had received as an apprentice on the *People's Advocate*. Contributions from talented writers like John E. Bruce (who wrote under the name Bruce Grit) and Ida B. Wells (under the name Iola) also kept the paper out of the red. The *Freeman's* poetry column, which often featured Fortune's own verses, also fed readership. But soon Fortune's political stance once again proved disastrous: After he endorsed Democratic candidate Grover Cleveland for president in 1888, Fortune's popularity flickered precariously. To keep his enterprise alive, Fortune took on a completely new editorial board, stopped lashing out quite so vehemently against Republicans, and renamed the paper the *New York Age*. With a new direction and a stable of great writers, the *New York Age* became highly respected and quickly gained national recognition. Gertrude B. Mossell, Fred. R. Moore, and W. E. B. Dubois all had their literary roots in the *New York Age*. When it ceased publication in 1960, the *New York Age* was the longest continuously running black-owned newspaper in American history.

The poems in *Voices Beyond Bondage* were selected from 36 separate 19th-century black-owned newspapers. Samuel Cornish, David Ruggles, Frederick Douglass, David Young, Louis Charles Roudanez, and Timothy Thomas Fortune were the most prominent publishers to contribute to the black-owned press and carry the torch of the poetry tradition. But, in the belief that every contribution to the early black-owned press was significant and deepened the literary tradition, poems were included in *Voices Beyond Bondage* from a host of smaller papers with less-famous editors. The collective efforts of these pioneering editors have been too often overlooked but their work, bravery, and dedication indelibly shaped American history. As this volume's editors, it has been our privilege and pleasure to reexamine and reintroduce these writings.

The Newspapers of Voices Beyond Bondage

In the index below, newspapers have been listed in alphabetical order. Cross-entry notes indicate when newspapers evolved from previous publications or evolved into subsequent publications.

The Afro-American Advance—Published in Minneapolis in 1899 but folded in 1900. This newspaper was formed by the merging of two newspapers, the *Colored Citizen* and the *Twin-City American.*

The American Citizen—Published somewhat sporadically in Baltimore from 1879 through the mid-1880s by J. W. Stokeley and Daniel Williams, its motto was "Africa's friends, Our friends; Her enemies, Our enemies."

The Anglo-African Magazine—A subsidiary publication of the *Weekly Anglo-African*, it was published sporadically while its parent paper was in print.

The Benevolent Banner—A pamphlet published in 1887 in North Topeka, Kansas, by Barker, Garrett & Co. This small publication lasted only one year.

The Christian Recorder—Originally started in 1854 by the African Methodist Episcopal Church under the editorship of John P. Campbell, but this early edition failed. The newspaper was resurrected in 1861 under the editorship of Elisha Weaver, and quickly became successful. Still in publication today, it is the longest non-continuously running black-owned newspaper ever published.

The Colored American—Previously *The Weekly Advocate,* this newspaper was published in 1837 in New York City by Philip Bell and Samuel Cornish; it ran until 1841. The paper marketed itself as "designed to be the organ of Colored Americans—to be looked on as their own, and devoted to their interests…"

The Concordia Eagle—Published in 1873 by David Young. This influential and highly successful paper ran for nearly two decades, folding in 1890. It's original motto was "Equal Rights to All Men."

Douglass' Monthly—Started in 1859 as a monthly supplement to the weekly *Frederick Douglass' Paper*, which folded in 1860. *Douglass' Monthly* continued through 1863. The *Monthly*'s masthead quoted *Ecclesiastes*: "Open thy mouth for the dumb, in the cause of all such as are appointed to destruction; open thy mouth, judge righteously, and plead the cause of the poor and needy."

Frederick Douglass' Paper—Started in 1851 when Douglass merged the *North Star* with Gerrit Smith's *Liberty Party Paper*. Based in Rochester, this wide reaching and highly popular newspaper was one of the most fierce antislavery publications ever produced. It ran until 1860.

Freedom's Advocate—Published in Washington, Ohio in 1829 by J. S. Pereman, it lasted almost two years. This newspaper resurfaced briefly in 1842, but only a few issues were produced before the newspaper again folded.

Freedom's Journal—Published in New York City in 1827 by Peter Williams Jr., John B. Russwurm, and Samuel Cornish, it was the first African American newspaper in the nation. This groundbreaking publication lasted two years.

Freedom's Press—Printed sporadically as a pamphlet in New York in 1842. Its publisher remained anonymous.

Historic Times—Published in Lawrence, Kansas, in 1891, this tiny newspaper ceased publication in less than six months.

The Independent—Started in 1854 by an anonymous group of African Americans; it was the longest running black-owned pamphlet ever produced. Although publication was sporadic, the pamphlet remained in circulation until 1885.

Kansas Herald—Published in Topeka in 1880. This short-lived newspaper billed itself as "The Only Colored Journal Published in Kansas." Also known as the *Kansas Weekly Herald*, and the *Herald of Kansas*.

The Louisville Newspaper—Started in 1849 in Kentucky as an underground pamphlet for and by African Americans. It came out sporadically over the course of two years; only six copies have survived.

The Loyal Georgian—Edited by John T. Shuften and originally founded in 1866 under the name *Colored American*. (Not to be confused with Bell's/Cornish's 1837 publication, *The Colored American*.) The newspaper was soon renamed the *Loyal Georgian* and ran through 1868.

Mirror of Liberty—Published in New York City by David Ruggles from 1838 to 1840. The paper pledged to "fearlessly attack vice and immorality, in high places and in low places."

The Missionary Record—Published in Charleston, South Carolina 1868–1879. Devoted to "the interest of free labor and general reform," this newspaper established itself as a strong local news source at a time marked by increasing hostility towards African Americans in South Carolina.

National Baptist World—Published in Wichita, Kansas, in 1894 as the *Baptist Headlight*, the paper was renamed that same year and ran under the motto "In the Interest of the Negro Baptist Church and the Race."

The Negro World—Published in Knoxville by James G. Patterson in 1884; it came out sporadically through 1891.

The New Orleans Tribune—Begun during the Civil War in 1864 by Dr. Louis Charles Roudanez. This was the first daily produced by a black-owned press, and was the first major black-owned newspaper to have both English and French editions. It ran continuously 1864-1868 and again 1869-1870.

The New York Age—Originally the *New York Freeman*, from 1884 until renamed in 1887, this newspaper was founded by T. Thomas Fortune and quickly gained national recognition. The *New York Age* ran uninterrupted until 1960; at the time of its closing it was the longest continuously-running black-owned publication ever produced.

The New York Freeman—Founded in 1884 by T. Thomas Fortune, this four-page weekly ran through 1887 when it expanded and became the *New York Age*.

The New York Globe—Published in New York City and edited by T. Thomas Fortune in 1880. This newspaper made a strong entry into the market but the paper folded in 1884, thanks largely to Fortune's radical politics. However, that same year Fortune rebuilt the paper and renamed it the *New York Freeman*.

The North Star—Started in 1847 by three prominent African American activists: William Cooper Nell, Martin Delany, and Frederick Douglass. This paper was a major journalistic force but folded in 1851. Its masthead proclaimed "Right Is of No Sex—Truth Is of No Color—God Is the Father of Us All, and We Are All Brethren." It was later merged with Gerrit Smith's *Liberty Party Paper* to become *Frederick Douglass' Paper*.

The Northern Star and Freeman's Advocate—Published by an anonymous group of African Americans in Albany in 1842-1843. This small paper proposed to "advocate the cause of temperance and reform and the equal rights of man, and to disseminate education among the colored portion of community."

The Palladium of Liberty—Published weekly in Columbus and distributed throughout the eastern states. Owned and edited by David Jenkins, this newspaper began in 1843 and ceased publication the following year.

The Richmond Planet—Founded in 1882 by thirteen former slaves from Richmond, the Planet was initially edited by Edmund A. Randolph. Two years later John Mitchell, Jr. succeeded Randolph and retained editorship until 1929; the *Planet* continued until 1938.

The Rights of All—Published in New York City in 1829 by Samuel E. Cornish, it lasted about a year. The motto of this eight-page publication was "Righteous Exaleth A Nation, Sin is a Reproach to Any People."

The Savannah Weekly Echo—Published in Savannah in 1883 by the Harden Brothers & D. Griffin under the motto "Onward and Upward." It ceased publication in late 1886.

The Union—Published in New Orleans in 1862; it was also called *L'Union* because it served the French/English speaking community. *The Union* ceased publication in 1864.

The Weekly Advocate—Started in 1837 by Philip Bell. Six months later, Samuel Cornish joined Bell's efforts and they renamed the paper the *Colored American*.

The Weekly Anglo-African—Published in New York City in 1859 by Thomas Hamilton, its motto ferociously proclaimed "Man Must Be Free; If Not

Through Law, Then Above The Law." The paper, also known simply as the *Anglo-African*, ceased publication in 1865.

The Weekly Defiance—Published in Atlanta in 1881 by William Pledger and J. H. Brown; it ceased publication in 1889.

Western Cyclone—Published in Nicodemus, Kansas, in 1886 by Arthur G. Tallman. It was renamed *Nicodemus Cyclone* in 1888 but folded that same year.

ALPHABET OF SLAVERY.

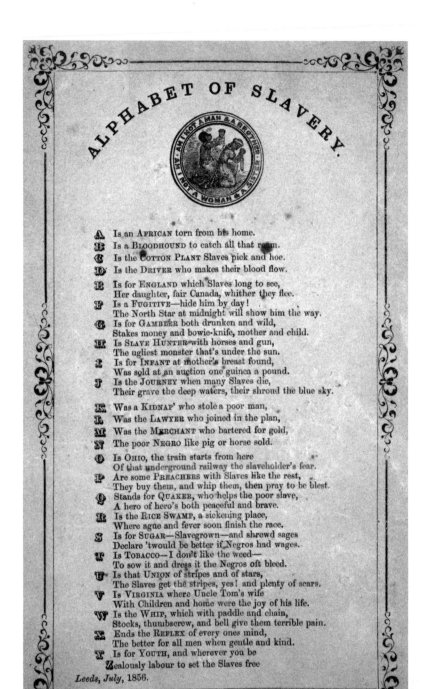

A Is an AFRICAN torn from his home.

B Is a BLOODHOUND to catch all that roam.

C Is the COTTON PLANT Slaves pick and hoe.

D Is the DRIVER who makes their blood flow.

E Is for ENGLAND which Slaves long to see,
Her daughter, fair Canada, whither they flee.

F Is a FUGITIVE—hide him by day!
The North Star at midnight will show him the way.

G Is for GAMBLER both drunken and wild,
Stakes money and bowie-knife, mother and child.

H Is SLAVE HUNTER with horses and gun,
The ugliest monster that's under the sun.

I Is for INFANT at mother's breast found,
Was sold at an auction one guinea a pound.

J Is the JOURNEY when many Slaves die,
Their grave the deep waters, their shroud the blue sky.

K Was a KIDNAP' who stole a poor man,

L Was the LAWYER who joined in the plan,

M Was the MERCHANT who bartered for gold,

N The poor NEGRO like pig or horse sold.

O Is OHIO, the train starts from here
Of that underground railway the slaveholder's fear.

P Are some PREACHERS with Slaves like the rest,
They buy them, and whip them, then pray to be blest.

Q Stands for QUAKER, who helps the poor slave,
A hero of hero's both peaceful and brave.

R Is the RICE SWAMP, a sickening place,
Where ague and fever soon finish the race.

S Is for SUGAR—Slavegrown—and shrewd sages
Declare 'twould be better if Negros had wages.

T Is TOBACCO—I don't like the weed—
To sow it and dress it the Negros oft bleed.

U Is that UNION of stripes and of stars,
The Slaves get the stripes, yes! and plenty of scars.

V Is VIRGINIA where Uncle Tom's wife
With Children and home were the joy of his life.

W Is the WHIP, which with paddle and chain,
Stocks, thumbscrew, and bell give them terrible pain.

X Ends the REFLEX of every ones mind,
The better for all men when gentle and kind.

Y Is for YOUTH, and wherever you be

Z Zealously labour to set the Slaves free

Leeds, July, 1856.

J. Kershaw and Son, Printers.

I

Bondage &
Calls to Freedom

Freedom

By B. B.
Freedom's Journal, September 7, 1827

My harp has long neglected laid,
And very little music made;
My Muse, at length, has fann'd the fire,
And *Freedom* sweet attunes my lyre.

FREEDOM's embalm'd in every heart,
And oh! how loath with it we part!
Purs'd by all, by all desir'd,
Caress'd by all, by all admir'd!

FREEDOM's the statesman's proudest boast,
And she's the patriotic toast;
She is the theme of all the sage,
And beautifies the poet's page.

FREEDOM nerves the warrior's arm,
Amid, the din of Mars' alarm,
'Tis this that cheers the martial band,
Contending for their natal land.

FREEDOM's the nurse of Science fair,
And fosters genius bright and rare;
She places man on equal ground,
Strews peace and plenty all around.

O, FREEDOM, fair goddess of peace!
Appear, and oppression shall cease;
O, listen, O, pity and see!
O, speak, and the *slave* shall be *free*.

The Tears of a Slave

By Africus
Freedom's Journal, March 14, 1828

Adieu, to my dear native shore,
To toss on the boisterous wave;
To enjoy my kindred no more,
But to weep—the tears of a SLAVE!

By the sons of freemen I'm borne,
To the land of the free and the brave;
From my wife and children I'm torn,
To weep—the sad tears of a SLAVE!

When, I think on mother and friends,
And the joy their countenance gave;
Ah! how my sad bosom it rends,
While weeping—the tears of a SLAVE!

Ah! now, I must labour for gold,
To pamper the pride of the knave;
Ah! now, I am shackled and sold
To weep—the sad tears of a SLAVE!

Keen sorrow so presses my heart,
That often I sigh for my grave;
While feeling the lash-cruel smart!
And weeping—the tears of a SLAVE!

Ye sons, of the free and the wise,
Your tender compassions I crave;
Alas! can your bosoms despise
The pitiful tears of a SLAVE!

Can a land of Christians so pure!
Let demons of slavery rave!
Can the angel of mercy endure,
The pitiless—tears of a SLAVE!

Just Heaven, to thee I appeal;
Hast thou not the power to save?
In mercy thy power reveal,
And dry—the sad tears of a SLAVE.

Slavery

By a Carolinian Slave named George Horton

By George M. Horton [Chatham County, North Carolina]
Freedom's Journal, July 18, 1828

When first my bosom glowed with hope,
I gaz'd as from a mountain top
      On some delightful plain;
But oh! how transient was the scene—
It fled as though it had not been,
      And all my hopes were vain.

How oft this tantalizing blaze
Has led me through deception's maze;
      My friend became my foe—
Then like a plaintive dove I mourn'd,
To bitter all my sweets were turn'd,
      And tears began to flow.

Why was the dawning of my birth
Upon this vile accursed earth,
      Which is but pain to me?
Oh! that my soul had winged its flight,
When first I saw the morning light,
      To worlds of liberty!

Come, melting Pity from afar
And break this vast, enormous bar
      Between a wretch and thee;
Purchase a few short days of time,

And bid a vassal rise sublime
On wings of liberty.

Is it because my skin is black,
That thou should'st be so dull and slack,
And scorn to set me free?
Then let me hasten to the grave,
The only refuge for the slave,
Who mourns for liberty.

The wicked cease from trouble there;
No more I'd languish or despair—
The weary there can rest?
Oppression's voice is heard no more,
Drudg'ry and pain, and toil are o'er,
Yes! there I shall be blest.

The African's Dream

The Colored American, April 3, 1841

There were bright visions in my dreams,
     Sights of my native land—
How beautiful her bonny streams,
     Flowing o'er golden sand—
How beautiful the flowers beside,
Stooping to drink their silver tide.

My old companions bounding came
     From bamboo huts and bowers,
To press my hand and call my name,
     And talk of boyhood's hours—
And there was one, my country's pride,
My heart seemed bursting when she died.

That wife, the faithful and the fair,
     Came with her lovely face—
With well known voice, and cheerful air
     She rushed to my embrace,
And pressed my lips, while smiles and tears
Stole from my heart the grief of years.

Brothers and sisters, kindred, all,
     With the sweet voice and eye,
Welcomed the lost one from his thrall,
     To native land and sky;
Their tears of pity, fast and warm,

Fell as they marked my scar-wreathed form.

Why did ye wake me from my sleep,
       To unavailing tears!
My heart is o'er the mighty deep,
       Mid scenes of other years:
Better that I had waked no more,
Or died upon my own bright shore.

Well, I shall weep—and toil—and die!
       Then, when my soul is free,
How quickly will it soar and fly
       My native land, to thee!
There I shall roam as free as air,
With the loved ones that wait me there.

The Northern Star

By S. F. B.
The Northern Star and Freeman's Advocate, February 3, 1842

Star of the North, whose placid ray,
Beamed mildly o'er yon sacred hill,
While whispering zephyrs seemed to say,
As silence slept and earth was still—
All hail, thou harbinger of gospel light!
Dispel the shades of natural lights,
And wake to ecstasy thy hands.
Sweet cherubs hail thy rising ray
And sing the dawn of gospel day!
Shine, lovely star! on every clime,
For bright thy peerless beauties be;
Gild with thy beam the wing of time,
And shed thy rays from sea to sea;
Then shall the world from darkness rise
And advocate the freeman's cause!

Song of the American Eagle

By A Lady of Vermont [Brandon, Vermont]
The North Star, January 7, 1848

I build my nest on the mountain's crest,
Where the wild winds rock my eaglets to rest;
Where the lightnings flash and the thunders crash,
And the roaring torrents foam and dash:
       For my spirit free henceforth shall be,
       A type for the sons of Liberty.

Aloft I fly, from my eyrie high,
Through the vaulted dome of the azure sky;
On a sunbeam bright take my airy flight,
And float in flood of liquid light:
       For I love to play in the noontide ray,
       And bask in a blaze from the throne of Day.

Away I spring, with a tireless wing,
On the feathery cloud I poise and swing;
I dart down the steep where the lightning leap,
And the clear blue canopy slowly sweep:
       For dear to me is the revelry
       Of a free and fearless Liberty.

I love the land where the mountains stand,
Like the watchtowers high of a patriot band:
For I may not hide, in my glory and pride,
Though the land be ever so fair and wide,
       Where Luxury reigns o'er voluptuous plains,

And fetters the freeborn soul in chains.

Then give to me in my flight to see
The land of the pilgrims ever free;
And I ne'er will rove from the haunts I love,
But watch, from my sentinel track above,
Your banner free over land and sea,
And exult in your glorious destiny.

Oh, guard ye well the land where I dwell,
Lest to future times the tale I tell,
When slow expires in smoldering fires
The goodly heritage of your sires,
How Freedom's light rose clear and bright
From fair Columbia's beacon-height,
Till ye quenched the flame in a starless night.

Then will I tear from your pennon fair
The stars ye set in triumph there!
My olive branch on the blast I'll launch,
The flattering stripes from the flag-staff wrench!
And away I'll flee, for I scorn to see
A craven race in the land of the free.

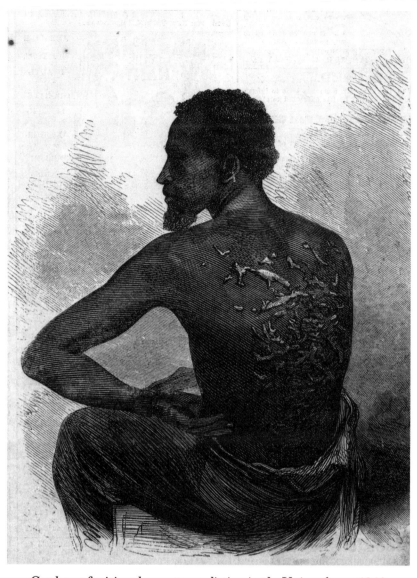

Gordon, a fugitive slave, upon enlisting in the Union Army; 1863

Voices Beyond Bondage

The Fugitive

"If thou mayest be free, use it rather." (I Corinthians, 7:21, KJV)

By W. G. H.
The North Star, January 21, 1848

Quick, fly to thy covert, thou hunted of men!
For the bloodhounds are laying o'er mountain and glen;
The riders are mounted, the loose rein is given,
And cures of wrath are ascending to heaven.
Oh! speed to thy footsteps, for ruin and death,
Like the hurricane's rage, gather thick round thy path;
And the deep muttered curses grow loud and more loud,
As horse after horse swells the thundering crowd.

Speed, speed, to thy footsteps! thy track has been found;
Now, sport for the *rider*, and blood for the *hound!*
Through brake and through forest the man-prey is driven;
Oh! help for the hopeless, thou merciful Heaven.
On! on to the mountain! they're baffled again,
And hope for the woe-stricken still may remain;
The fast-flagging steeds are all white with their foam;
The blood-hounds have turned from the chase to their home.

Joy! joy to the wrong'd one! the haven he gains,
Escaped from his thralldom, and freed from his chains,
The heaven-stamped image—the God-given soul
No more shall the spoiler at pleasure control.
O, shame to Columbia, that on her bright plains
Man pines in his fetters, and curses his chains!
Shame! shame! that her star-spangled banner should wave,

Where the lash is made red in the blood of the slave.

Sons of old "Pilgrim fathers!" and are ye thus dumb?
Shall tyranny triumph, and freedom succumb?
While mothers are torn from their children apart,
And agony sunders the cords of the heart?
Shall the sons of those sires that once spurned the chain,
Turn bloodhounds to hunt down the captive again?
O, shame to your honor, and shame to your pride,
And shame on your memory ever abide!

Will not your old sires start up from the ground,
At the crack of the whip, and bay of the hound,
And shaking their skeleton hands in your face,
Cursed the germs that produced such a miscreant race?
O, rouse thee for freedom, before on our path
Heaven pours without mixture the vials of wrath!
Unloose every burden—break off every chain—
Restore to the bondman his freedom again.

Then shall Mercy, delighted, look down from above,
And smile to behold us, a nation of love;
And silenced for aye over mountain and glen,
Shall be the wild shout of the hunters of men.
Here righteousness shall in abundance be given,
Like the plenteous showers descending from heaven,
And angels descending, will herald again,
Peace, peace, upon earth, good-will towards men.

The North Star

By S. S. W. [Battle Creek, Missouri]
The North Star, January 28, 1848

Oh, hark! what voice the silence breaks?
What accents new are those we hear?
List, freeman, 'tis a *chattel* speaks!—
A *chattel's* voice salutes your ear.
Bursting the bonds that him confined,
From darkness sprung a giant mind;
Yes, he's escaped from Slavery's den,
And guides the NORTH STAR with his pen.

Hail, beam-light of liberty!
With joy we greet thy ray afar,
And pray that thou mayest ever be
Freedom's unchanging polar star.
We long had looked upon the skies,
To see the Star of Hope arise,
And shed upon the bleeding slave,
Its cheering ray this side the grave.

And, now, behold! far in the north,
Near where the Lion bears his sway,
A brilliant Star is beaming forth,
Cheering the down-trod with its ray.
It shines upon the fugitive;
It bids the slave take heart and live;
For soon—ah! soon, may come the day,
When he shall bask in Freedom's ray.

Unchanged, unchanging, ever shine,
      On this benighted land of ours;
Until the force of Truth divine
      Shall break the proud oppressor's powers:
Till man shall walk the verdant sod,
In the blest image of his God,
Free and untrammelled—then thy ray
May well be lost in Freedom's day.

In this piece the North Star is an allegory for Frederick Douglass. While the North Star symbolized the guiding light on the journey northward for escaped slaves (such as Douglass), the North Star *was also the name of Douglass's first publication.*

God Never Made a Sin

By Theodore Doughty Miller
The Louisville Newspaper, February 10, 1849

Ah! dark skinned tribes, though black we be,
God, our creator, made us free;
To all He life and being gave,
But never, never made a slave.

His works, all wondrous to behold,
Proclaim to us a power untold;
He made the sea and formed the wave,
But never, never made a slave.

He made yon sun with a splendor bright,
The moon to brighten earth's dark night;
He made in power this vast concave,
But never, never made a slave.

He made all colors and all climes,
Of living things made every kind;
For all he made the common grave,
But never, never made a slave.

Though Adam's sin brought pain and death,
Yet life came with Christ's dying breath;
From henceforth heaven and hell may rave,
His blood speaks freedom to the slave.

For all He sent His Son to be
The Great High Priest of Liberty;
From sin's strong chains our souls to save,
And break the fetters of the slave.

All men are equal in His sight,
The bond, the free, the black, the white;
He made them all—all freedom gave—
God made the man, man made the slave.

But glorious tidings of great joy!
Yon kingdom beams without alloy;
And while we view that "crystal sea,"
We'll shout, praise God, we're free! we're free!

Anti-slavery broadside; circa 1805
(Collection of the New-York Historical Society; neg #77769d)

The Negro Girl

The Nashville American says a negro girl belonging to Louis C. Lisby,
committed suicide last week, to avoid giving information of her
mother's place of concealment, who ran away.

By Mrs. S. H. B. Smith
The North Star, July 20, 1849

And must my mother feel again
The dungeon rack, the crushing chain?
The stinging scourge, the bitter jeer,
Again fall on my tortured ear—
As all defenseless thou hast stood,
Beneath the infuriate lash—O, God!
And scarcely cared to lift on high
Thy look of speechless agony?

Thou who wast ever good and kind—
To duty all thy thoughts inclined—
Whose love has been the one bright ray,
Cheering my drear and toilsome way,
Before my tottering steps could stray
From the lone cabin where I lay,
And sobbed away the weary hours
Till thou shouldst come at shut of flowers;

Thy sultry tasks of daylight done,
To greet me, underneath the moon,
Stretching my arms in eager glee,
At the first sight I caught of thee,
Scarce turning from thy close embrace

To note gay buds which thou didst place
Within my hand—though dearly bought
The toys thy weary steps had sought.

And when my growing strength could share
Thy mid-day toils, if noon's hot glare
Fell on my shrinking head, how soon
Thy mother's heart has bid me come,
And smiled to see, me gently laid
Beneath the cool Magnolia's shade,
While thy own love-nerved arm has wrought
The double task, my rest that bought.

And O, when o'er me sickness came,
Unmindful of thy toil-spent frame,
Can I forget the tender care
Which seemed each pain to sooth and share?
I could have deemed it sweet to die
Beneath that soft, that loving eye,
While thou didst hold my fevered hand,
And whisper of the better land,
Bright visions, which no longer cheer
My darkened path of gloom and fear:

No! by thy love and by thy woes,
My mother, I can ne'er disclose
Thy refuge, though my spirits faint
At the strange pangs their threatening paint;
Yet I shall quail beneath the glance
On these stern eyes, whose look, perchance,
May read within my trembling breast,
The secret by no words confessed.

But unappalled, the death-closed ear,
Their fierce menacing tones may hear,
And no revealing word be wrung
From death's cold lip, and palsied tongue
O, it is fearful thus to die—
Yet, in that brighter world on high,
May some sweet angel plead for me,
Dear mother, that I died for thee!

Song of Brotherhood

By S. D. Anderson
The North Star, September 7, 1849

Brothers, sing! The chains are broken,
Hear the anthem, see the token,
Man's great heart at length has spoken—
    Hear it, Brothers, hear!
Listen to its songs of gladness!

Hark! from thrones and altars falling,
Hark! from bondage spirit-galling,
Freedom's voice is loudly calling—
    Hear it, Brothers, hear!
Liberty is in each breathing.

Noble hearts to life are waking,
'Neath the sunlight proudly breaking,
Error's troops are meanly quaking—
    Hear it, Brothers, hear!
Look and see the day is dawning.

All around old things are dying,
Force and fraud in terror flying,
Whilst for light the world is crying—
    Hear it, Brothers, hear!
Loud as tones of winter's tempest.

Hark! a voice across the water,
From each stricken son and daughter,

Mid the famine and the slaughter—
  Hear it, Brothers, hear!
They are talking too of freedom.

On the mountains they are telling
Thoughts that now in secret welling,
Soon will like a torrent swelling,
  Hear it, Brothers, hear!
For it tells you light is coming.

From that land where year on year,
Heard the lash and saw the tear,
Do some rays of light appear?
  Hear it, Brothers, hear!
Brotherhood is struggling upward.

Oh then, Brothers, with your armor,
Heed ye not the siren charmer,
See the battle wages warmer—
  Hear it, brother, hear!
Join your comrades in the contest.

The Youthful Captive

By Ellesbo
The Louisville Newspaper, February 1850

Securely chained to walls of stone,
Within a dungeon damp and low—
There ne'er was heard a friendly tone;
      A captive slept,
A youthful brow the captive bore,
And sadness deep his features wore,
For darksome clouds his spirit o'er
      Had rudely swept.

As daylight faded in the west,
All peaceful was the captive's rest,
No gloomy thoughts pervade his breast,
      Nor doubts—nor fears,
For back he wandered in his dreams,
To childhood's haunts and gliding streams,
When o'er him fell the silver gleams
      Of early years.

Again his mother's voice he heard,
Sweet as the carol of a bird,
With music fraught each gentle word,
      His heart made light—
As is in the blissful days of yore,
Ere grief had swept his spirit o'er,
A father's care was his once more,
      And all seemed bright.

In his sweet dreams of untold bliss,
Too holy for a world like this,
Upon his cheek a sister's kiss
                    He felt impressed;
A brother's hand again he grasped,
Which in his own he firmly clasped—
Through joyous scenes again he passed,
                    And he was blest!

With bounding heart and gladsome pride,
Once more he roamed the forest wide,
And climbed the rugged mountain's side,
                    As oft before
He'd done in young, glad, light-winged years,
When he knew not of sorrow's tears,
And dreamed not life had grief and fears
                    For him in store.

The Auction Block

By H. M. [Deerfield, New York]
Frederick Douglass' Paper, October 2, 1851

The sable Mother, child in hand, is now exposed to view;
Around her an unpitying hand, to nature all untrue;
Her form's surveyed, while ribald jests meet her offended ear,
Rude laugh, course wit, is echoed round, and this she has to bear.

The auctioneer attests her worth, and asks one hundred more,
"Without the Brat, I'd buy the Wench," exclaims a Southern boor.
His powerless arm her husband lifts, who grits his snowy teeth;
But quickly awed by stern command, he tries to choke his grief.

"Well! be it so," the owner cries—"come bid her off alone!"
She hears him not—but ah! the Father breathes a hollow groan.
Her piteous eyes are cast around, and suppliant she stands;
But "meek-eyed Pity" dwells not there, she lives in other lands.

Poor doom'd one, hark! the hammer falls, the wretch asserts his right,
He tears her from her Boy, to whom she clings with all her might.
"My child!" she screams—"in mercy buy my own, my darling boy!
Quick! buy him quick! You cannot sure my life blood thus destroy";

"And look! There stands my husband dear, a manly heart has he,
And willing hands—oh! buy him too, in mercy unto me!"
Alas! as well might victim plead with tiger on the plain,
As soon old Ocean yield to view the drowned alive again.

She seeks his eye—and reads her fate, what now on earth is left

to cheer that widowed childless one, of all but life bereft?
And what is life? she asks not it, she's torn from all away,
She prays for death—an early death—that sable one doth pray.

"The Parting: 'Buy Us, Too!'"; 1863

VOICES BEYOND BONDAGE

The Rescue of Jerry

The following spirited Poem, from the pen of G. W. Putnam was read at the recent glorious Celebration at Syracuse. Tune—Yankee Girl

By G. W. PUTNAM
Frederick Douglass' Paper, October 22, 1852

Morn comes in the East, and the world is awake,
And the bright sunshine gladdens the valley and lake;
The silver dew glistens on hillside and tree;
Afar o'er the mountains the rising mists flee;

Now the yeomen go forth for the fruits of the soil.
And the artisans hasten again to their toil;
But hark! the wild cry which comes forth on the air
Speaks of sadness and sorrow, of woe and despair,

How the blood moves apace, how the beating heart thrills,
As the low tolling bells echo out o'er the hills!
Haste! Haste! for the boaster hath set on his hounds,
And Oppression hath leaped o'er Humanity's bounds.

Lo! the wolves from their covert have scented their prey!
Their fetter is on him! they bear him away!
To his doom they will take him, o'er field and o'er flood,
And the Tyrant's keen lash will drink deep of his blood!

Up! up! to the rescue! O stalwart of limb!
From the salt-spring and cornfield, and workshop so dim,
Pass on the bright summons! and marshalled in might,
Come forth, O ye people, for Freedom and Right!

And their words like the voice of the ocean arouse,
As they murmured defiance and wrath to their foes.
"Say brothers! for this did the patriot toil?
For this did their life-blood once redden our soil"?

And the hunters of men stood aghast at the sound,
And trembled with fear as the watchword went round,
"Come peaceful deliverance—or bloody affray,
The Slave shall be free ere the dawning of day!"

It was evening—the stars kept their watch in the sky,
When through the still Heaven rang glorious and high
The cry of the PEOPLE—"Ho! down with the wall!
Bring him out! bring him forth! set him free from his thrall!"

Hark the crash! it was done! with the quickness of thought
'Mid the fire of the foe, in the path of the shot!
And the bright throng of Heaven bent downward to see,
When they brought forth the man, still in fetters, but FREE!

And the shout that went up as proud Tyranny fell,
Shook, with its deep thunder, the ramparts of Hell!
Bear him on by the altars unscarred by the chain,
Where the Trumpet of Freedom ne'er echoed in vain.

Where the Priest hath not taken the robber's reward,
Or the man-thief once drank of the cup of the Lord.
Where they ponder what God hath inscribed on the sky:
"Man is great and immortal! the truth cannot die!"

Where long hath been heard, through Faith's open door,
The dash of Time's wave on Eternity's shore.
Where was planted with tears 'mid the tempest of Sin
The germ of the harvest this night gathered in.

And still by the torch-light they bear him along,
With the words of rejoicing, with shout and with song,
And the young city won, in that hour's mighty strife,
An honor unfading—green laurels for life!

And pure hearted WOMEN, high beauty and worth,
To cheer on the deed and doers, came forth.
And to *him* whose transgression would stain ocean's flood,
They paid thirty pieces—the old price of blood![1]

And a Boaster's vain threat—and a Slave's *broken gyves*
Side by side have their place in the Nation's archives!
He is gone—with no brand of the Slave on his brow—
And the throne of a Monarch[2] shall shelter him now.

But Freemen, O keep ye forever and aye,
In honored remembrance the deed and the day!
And Life's coming host shall tell proudly the tale
How the plotters were baffled—the boasters grew pale,

When the might of a PEOPLE by Tyranny curst
Gave their threats to the winds—and their "LAW" to the dust!
And shall point where forever, on Time's record broad,
The lofty deed beareth the signet of God!

> *The "Jerry" of this poem is William "Jerry" Henry, a fugitive slave from Missouri who was living and employed in Syracuse. "Jerry" was arrested under the terms of the 1850 Fugitive Slave Act (a.k.a. the "Bloodhound Law"[3]), which required that free states and territories return captured fugitive slaves.*

---

1   The rescuers sent "Jerry's" owner thirty three-bit pieces of silver as restitution.
2   Refers to the British Crown. At the time of this writing, Canada was under British rule.
3   See notes in "To ******" and "To Mr. Fillmore" in the section *Dedications & Remembrances*.

to their owners. The arrest coincided with the Liberty Party's 1851 conven-tion. Appalled by the law and the arrest, Liberty party members stormed the prison where "Jerry" was held, and smuggled him to safety in Ontario. The "glorious Celebration at Syracuse" as referenced at the start of this poem was an abolitionist rally of some 1,500 attendees held on the anniversary of the of the rescue.

Untitled

By E. P. Rogers [Newark, New Jersey]
Frederick Douglass' Paper, June 10, 1853

"Loosed from your moorings you are free,
     But fast in chains am I;
You move before the gentle gale,
     Beneath the scourge I lie.

You fly around the mighty globe,
     You swift-winged angels be;
I am confined in iron bands,
     Oh, God, that I were free!

Oh! that I were on one of you,
     'Neath your protecting wing—
Upon your gallant decks no more
     To feel oppression's sting.

But ah! alas! 'twist me and you
     The turbid waves roll high,
Go on! go on! I'd gladly go
     Could I but swim or fly.

The ships are gone—they hide afar;
     I'm left in hottest hell,
Why was I born to be a brute
     With earthly friends to dwell?

Why am I thus a wretched slave?
　　Oh God deliver me!
Is there a God? thy power vouchsafe,
　　And let me now be free.

Oppression I will not endure—
　　I rather choose to die;
Come life, or death, I must be free,
　　God helping me I'll try."

When thus thy mighty spirit yearned,
　　The chains could not confine;
Thou didst resolve to strike the blow,
　　And Liberty was thine.

This piece is inspired by and is a direct takeoff of Frederick Douglass's "Chesapeake Bay" speech, as recorded in chapter ten of the Narrative of the Life of Frederick Douglass, an American Slave, Written by Himself. *In a note penned to Douglass and printed as an introduction to this poem, Roger writes, "Following, you will find, thrown into verse, your eloquent apostrophe to the ships on the Chesapeake Bay, while yet in bondage—Those soul-stirring words [. . .] have attracted the notice of thousands."*

The Fugitive's Soliloquy and Prayer
After His Rendition to Slavery

By Anonymous
Frederick Douglass' Paper, August 18, 1854

Farewell, freedom! farewell, pleasure!
    I must back to slavery go;
Toil to swell a master's treasure,
      Through a life of pain and woe.
        Palsied be the power which gave
        Back the *man* to be the slave!

Farewell, hope's inspiring feeling!
    Hope exists not for me now;
Only sad endurance, sealing
      Dullness on my soul and brow.
        Farewell, manhood's high employ,
        Manhood's aims, and manhood's joy!

Farewell, life! this is no living.
    Crushed by slavery's cursed chain,
Welcome, death! thy summons giving
      Life and liberty again.
        Those who reach thy ice-bound shore,
        Shall be rendered back no more.

Farewell, free, immortal spirit!
    Bought with priceless, dying love;
"Things" like me should not inherit

Treasures in the realms above.
Soul, farewell! Oh! Never crave
Union with this chattel slave.

Farewell, kindness! tender, loving;
Reign, O hatred, in my breast!
Every powerful motive moving
To do vengeance dire behest.
Let me scorn now and betray
These, my masters, as I may.

Yet, methinks, a voice is saying,
"Suffer! leave thy cause with me;
Cease thy wild, thy vain essaying,
To avenge thy misery.
Vengeance unto me belongs,
I will recompense thy wrongs."

With thine eyes, which never slumber,
Lord! behold and mark the whole;
Wrongs, no computation numbers,
To the body, to the soul.
Oh! avenge these cruel wrongs;
Vengeance unto God belongs.

Griefs are pressing me like mountains;
Stay these floods, my weeping eyes!
Back, ye tear drops! to your fountains;
Bursting heart! suppress thy sighs,
Impotent these signs to show
Half my seething, withering woe.

'Tis the Worst and the Best

"This bill is, at the same time, both the worst and the best bill ever acted upon by Congress." — Speech of Honorable Charles Sumner of Massachusetts, on the final passage of the Kansas and Nebraska bill.

BY THE WORKSHOP BARD [Marietta, Ohio]
Frederick Douglass' Paper, August 25, 1854

'Tis the worst and best of the deeds ye have done,
  And destiny's angel the records shall trace
It shall tell that the race of the traitors is run,
  And that freemen henceforth shall be found in their place.

From New Hampshire's tall peaks, frowning darkly and dun,
  To the valleys which sleep by the far Western Flood,
Shall be echoed the deeds of her recreant son,
  Who hath bartered in shame what was purchased with blood.

Too long, like the ravenous vultures of war,
  Have the traitors been fed, while our rights have been sold;
Those rights, which, to freemen, were dearer by far
  Than the gems of a crown in their settings of gold.

'Tis written! *Aye written!* For lo! on the wall,
  The pale finger of doom hath engraven it deep;
And a voice, which presages your ultimate fall,
  Is awakened at last, and shall never more sleep.

It shall thrill through the land, like a wail from the dead,
  And a voice shall reply from our forefather's graves,
That "the soil where the blood of the martyrs was shed,

Shall be evermore free from the footfall of slaves."

All hail to the Future! Its promise is ours,
      Though the storm and the tempest should herald its birth;
Ye shall look, but in vain, for a spirit that cowers;
      Ye shall learn, for a truth, that *there yet is a North!*

"'Tis the worst, and the best;" for abroad through the land,
      The pent fires of Freedom at last shall break forth;
And Liberty yet shall have whereon to stand,
      Till she shatters the thrones of the tyrants of earth!

This poem is written of the Kansas-Nebraska Act of 1854, which formed the territories of Kansas and Nebraska, respectively. Under the law, residents in each territory were to decide, by popular sovereignty, if slavery would be allowed therein. (See note in "Nebraska and Slavery" and "Southrons.") The Kansas-Nebraska Act effectively repealed the Missouri Compromise of 1820. Both pro- and anti-slavery advocates considered the Act a blow to their causes.

The Slave Auction

By Frances Ellen Watkins
Frederick Douglass' Paper, September 22, 1854

The sale began—young girls were there,
    Defenseless in their wretchedness,
Whose stifled sobs of deep despair
    Revealed their anguish and distress.

And mothers stood, with streaming eyes,
    And saw their dearest children sold;
Unheeded rose their bitter cries,
    While tyrants barter'd them for gold.

And woman, with her love and truth—
    For these in sable forms may dwell—
Gaz'd on the husband of her youth,
    With anguish none may paint or tell.

And men, whose sole crime was their hue,
    The impress of their Maker's hand,
And frail and shrinking children too,
    Were gathered in that mournful band.

Ye who have laid your lov'd to rest,
    And wept above their lifeless clay,
Know not the anguish of that breast,
    Whose lov'd are rudely torn away.

Ye may not know how desolate
    Are bosoms rudely forced to part,
And how a dull and heavy weight
    Will press the life drops from the heart.

A Southern slave auction; 1861

To the Slave

By G. W. PUTNAM
Frederick Douglass' Paper, November 10, 1854

Dark brow'd Brother, fear thou not;
Let hope forsake thy bosom never;
Widely known thy bleeding lot;
Trust thou in thy God forever,
Burning tongues thy woes are telling,
Manly forms for thee are kneeling,
Manly hearts for thee are swelling,
Slavery's knell is pealing,
And a voice cries, "Fear thou not,
Raise the heart within thee drooping;
God the slave has not forgot;
Omnipotence is stooping!"

Dark brow'd Mother, fear thou not:
God for thee has spoken;
Thine offspring have been sold and bought;
Earth's silver cords been broken.
Those whom thy warm love have shared;
To thee the sum of all earth's charms;
All the scourge and chain have spared,
Shall leaping find thine arms.

Dark brow'd Sister, fear thou not,
In thy house of bondage pining;
Thee woman's heart hath not forgot,
Her arms are round thee twining.

Her ear hath heard thy moaning sigh,
With glance of fire her kindling eye.
While recreant priest was dreaming:
Hath seen the tyrant bind thy form,
And with thy life-blood, rich and warm,
His scourge accursed streaming;
Then raised to heaven that tear dimmed eye,
Nor faltering at the priesthood's nod;
Midst jeer and laugh, hath sent on high
A woman's prayer to God.

O poor wronged bondman, fear thou not;
God thinks upon the slave;
The hand which holds the worlds I wot
Is strong indeed to save.
For He hath seen thy trampled soul,
Whose fires divine would gladly burn,
Not palsied by sin's maddening bowl.
Beyond His yearning call—"Return."
Quick with immortal life to feel,
Not dead beyond the spirit's call,
And covered o'er with death's dark pall,
But crushed beneath a *human* heel!
A price was paid for that wronged soul,
When Truth and Mercy met,
Though broken, He can make it whole,
Though low, can raise it yet.
To join its voice in triumph song,
To take the joys which God hath given,
To barter the stern tyrant's wrong,
For fullness of reward in Heaven.
And bid it speed towards its high goal,
When at the trumpet's piercing blast,
A blighted and a burning scroll

Yon firmament hath passed!

O bound and bleeding, fear ye not!
Heaven's light for you is breaking,
With power of God's right arm begot
The wide earth is awaking!
Though Oppression's angry ocean
Rages on in wild commotion;
Yet above the darkened wave,
Cheering every heart forlorn,
Like a pale light o'er a grave,
Gleams the moral dawn.
And again the thrilling cry
Judea's startled deserts heard,
Rings along our northern sky!
Nearer it comes—and blest are they
Who make their hearts the Lord's highway,
And listen to His word.

The Cry of the American Slave

By H. G. A.
Frederick Douglass' Paper, April 20, 1855

There's a promise of freedom
    For me and for mine;
I hear the glad tidings,
    I see the light shine;
But it shineth afar yet,
    The hill-tops are bright,
While the vale where the slave lies
    Is gloomy as night;
And the voice of deliv'rance
    Sounds faint, where the cries
And the groans of the scourged
    And the fettered arise.

Press on, my white brothers!
    The tyrants are strong,
Ye have giants to cope with—
    Oppression and Wrong;
Be brave, my white brothers!
    Your work is of love;
All good men pray for you,
    And God is above;
And the poor slave he crieth
    Unto ye for aid—
O, be not discouraged!
    O, be not afraid!

From the cotton plantation,
　　　The rice swamp, the mill,
The cane field, the workshop,
　　　The cry cometh still—
O! save us, and shield us,
　　　We groan and we faint;
No words can our sorrows,
　　　Our miseries paint.
Our souls are our masters',
　　　They sport with our Lives,
They torture and scourge us
　　　With whips and with gyves.

We see scowling faces
　　　On every hand,
We bear on our persons
　　　The marks of the brand;
We're fed, and we're cared for,
　　　Like horses and hogs;
We're cut and we're shot at,
　　　And hunted with dogs;
Like goods we are bartered,
　　　And given and sold;
And the rights of our race
　　　There are none to uphold—

Save *ye*, noble workers
　　　In Freedom's great cause;
Save *ye*, loud proclaimers,
　　　Of God's righteous laws,
Who call us your brothers,
　　　Though black be our skin,
And own we have hearts
　　　These dark bosoms within—

Like feelings, emotions,
      And passions, with those
Who spurn us, and scorn us,
      And scoff at our woes.

O! press on, and hasten
      The good coming time,
When the hue of the skin
      Shall no more be a crime;
When a man, though a Negro,
      May fearless give birth
To his thoughts, and his hopes,
      With the proudest on earth;
When no master shall own him,
      Nor tear him apart
From the wife of his bosom,
      The child of his heart.

I *know* the time's coming,
      I'm *sure* 'twill be here,
For the voice of a prophet
      Hath sung in mine ear—
"Make ready the way
      For the advent of Him,
In whose presence the splendors
      Of earth shall grow dim;
All pride shall be humbled,
      Oppression shall cease,
And men, like true brethren,
      Shall sojourn in peace."

I see the faint glimmer
      Of light;—shall these eyes
Behold the bright sun

In its glory arise?
Shall these hands grasp the freedom
        For which I and mine,
In the depths of our misery,
        Languish and pine?
Life waneth apace—
        I am feeble and cold—
O, hasten to snatch me
        From Slavery's hold!

Our Countrymen in Chains; 1837

VOICES BEYOND BONDAGE

The Nameless People

By Vagante
Frederick Douglass' Paper, June 1, 1855

Smitten and branded and manacled,
  A homeless and nameless nation,
Unstoried, despised by the centuries,
  Crouched in dull adoration
Beside our temples and palaces,
  And stoopeth its neck to our tread.
Stolid, untutored and languageless,
  It utters no love, no anger,
But grindeth in hopeless apathy,
  Or drowseth in brutish languor,
'Mid harvests and treasures, whose lordliness
  It claimeth less than the dead.

Aliens and foemen by heritage,
  We bar them afar from our slumber;
We clog them with statutes of jealousy,
  We muse if they gather in number;
Beside us, yet stricken with banishment!
  Among us, yet foreign in soul!
The patriot seeketh no sympathy
  In them for his country's glory:
The statesmen hopes in their brutishness,
  When he ponders our coming story;
We smother the anthems of liberty
  Which over their cabins might roll.

A shadow behind our prosperity,
  A menacing spectre, though humble;
A mute, mysterious prophecy,
  Their multitudes murmur and mumble
A spell o'er our nation's futurity,
  Which dies ere it reaches our ken.
What shall the ending be?—Bitterness?
  Shall these helot millions ever
Stand humbly aside from humanity?—
  No shattering exodus sever
Their bonds?—No fatal necessity
  Destroy them, or blazon them men?

Shall this Samson, sightless with ignorance,
  And dungeoned in servile terror,
Ne'er bow in our temple of selfishness
  Against its columns of error,
And make it a hideous sepulchre,
  Entombing his shame and our might?
What wind shall quicken the skeletons,
  And flesh them for lust and slaughters?
Guard well, O lordly posterity!
  Thy treasures, thy delicate daughters!
Keep arms within grasping! Set sentinels!
  The spoiler may come in the night.

No! we will wander, like Israel,
  Through waters yawning, but holden;
No wheels shall fall from our chariots;
  We will bribe Jehovah with golden
Fanes. No MENES shall desecrate
  The beautiful walls of our pride.
O! soothe us with flattering oracles;
  Cast horoscopes starry with splendor;

Muffle the footsteps of Destiny;
　　　Brand the prophet of God and offender;
Let us hasten to die: Futurity
　　　Hath secrets of horror to hide.

Nebraska and Slavery

By Jessie Elwood
The Independent, February 1857

Our wide, our fair, our happy land!
Franchised from scorned oppression's band;
"Equal and free" our people stand;
Proudly earth's homage they demand,
And call her thralled, on every hand,
   To liberty, blest Liberty!

But, list! back comes a gathered sound
From Europe's nations, fetter-bound—
From every tribe the wide world round;
"In all *our* realms is nothing found,
No blight, no curse, above the ground,
   Like slavery! *your* slavery."

Again our prayer to God we send,
His kingdom may on earth descend;
And to the earth's remotest end
Our yearning charities extend;
Calling the nations all to bend
   To laws of love and equity.

But back returns a smothered cry
From where Pacific's islands lie;
Ah! yes, from Afric, swelling high;
From every land beneath the sky:
"Heaven shield us from *your* equity,

Your love, your curse, your slavery!"

Yet still we hail the world to view
Our boundless wealth of azure blue,
Of forest green; streams wander through!
From crowded dotage, call the true
To come and breathe of life anew,
        In youth and hale posterity.

And shall that hideous monster crawl,
Stretch forth its fangs, and shed its pall
O'er soil unstained, empoisoning all
Where free winds play? For curses call
'Neath setting suns this ruin fall,
        This sum of sins, foul slavery!

Oh! Ye who for the truth are strong!
Think not that justice lingereth long!
Pity the sin-bound, sin-sold throng!
Know right must triumph over wrong,
And earth soon sing her paean song
        To love, to truth, and equity.

While slavery was never legal in the Nebraska territory, it was never expressly illegal, either. The territory was formed in 1854 by the Kansas-Nebraska Act (see notes in "'Tis the Worst and the Best" and "Southrons"), which allowed the two territories to decide by popular vote whether slavery would be allowed; Nebraska never voted on the issue. Slavery as an institution did not exist in the territory, but slave owners who had purchased slaves while living in slaveholding states were allowed to bring slaves with them into Nebraska as property.

Be Active

By Frances Ellen Watkins
The Weekly Anglo-African, July 30, 1859

Onward, onward, sons of freedom,
    In the great and glorious strife;
You've a high and holy mission
    On the battle field of life.

See oppression's feet of iron
    Grind a brother to the ground,
And from bleeding heart and bosom,
    Gapeth many a fearful wound.

Sit not down with idle pity,
    Gazing on his mighty wrong;
Hurl the bloated tyrant from him—
    Say my brother, oh, be strong!

See that sad, despairing mother
    Clasp her burning brow in pain;
Lay your hand upon her fetters—
    Rend, oh! rend her galling chain!

Here's a pale and trembling maiden,
    Brutal arms around her thrown;
Christian father, save, oh! save her,
    By the love you bear your own!

Yearly lay a hundred thousand
        New-born babes on Moloch's[4] shrine;
Crush these gory, reeking altars—
        Christians, let this work be thine.

Where the Southern roses blossom,
        Weary lives go out in pain,
Dragging to death's shadowy portals,
        Slavery's heavy galling chain.

Men of every clime and nation,
        Every faith, and sect, and creed,
Lay aside your idle jangling,
        Come and staunch the wounds that bleed.

On my people's blighted bosom,
        Mountain weights of sorrow lay;
Stop not now to ask the question,
        Who shall roll the stone away?

Set to work the moral forces,
        That are yours of church and state;
Teach them how to war and battle
        'Gainst oppression, wrong, and hate.

Oh! be faithful! Oh! be valiant,
        Trusting, not in human might;
Know that in the darkest conflict,
        God is on the side of right!

---

4   In the Old Testament, Moloch was a Canaanite god to whom children were sacri-
    ficed.

The Dying Fugitive

By Frances Ellen Watkins
The Anglo-African Magazine, August 1859

Slowly o'er his darkened features,
    Stole the warning shades of death;
And we knew the shadowing angel
    Waited for his parting breath.

He had started for his freedom,
    And his heart beat firm and high—
But before he won the guerdon,
    Came the message—he must die.

He must die, when just before him,
    Lay the long'd for, precious prize—
And the hopes that lit him onward,
    Faded out before his eyes.

For a while a fearful madness,
    Rested on his weary brain;
And he thought, the hateful tyrant,
    Had rebound his galling chain.

Then he raved in bitter anguish—
    "Take me where that good man dwells!"
For a name to freedom precious
    Lingered 'mid life's shattered cells.

But as sunshine gently stealing,
   O'er the storm cloud's gloomy track—
Through the tempests of his bosom,
   Came the light of reason back.

And without a sigh or murmur,
   For the home he'd left behind,
Calmly yielded lie his spirit,
   To the Father of mankind.

Thankful that so near to freedom,
   He with eager steps had trod—
E'er his ransomed spirit rested;
   On the bosom of his God.

The Slave

By William Wells Brown
The Weekly Anglo-African, February 1860

Wide over the tremulous sea
    The moon spread her mantle of light,
And the gale, gently dying away,
    Breathed soft on the bosom of night.

By the sea-side, a panting slave stood,
    And poured forth his pitiful tale;
His tears were unseen in the flood,
    His sighs were unheard in the gale.

"Ah! wretch!" in wild anguish he cried,
    "From friends and from liberty torn!
Ah! Alfred! Would thou hadst died,
    Before from thy home thou wert borne!

Through groves at pleasure I strayed,
    Love and hope made my bosom their home;
There I talked with my wife and my babe,
    Nor thought of the anguish to come.

From thicket the man-stealer sprang,
    My cry echoed loud through the air;
There was nothing but death in his eye,
    He was cold to the tones of despair.

But hark! in the silence of night,
      The voices of loved ones I hear,
And sadly, beneath the wan light,
      I see their fair forms drawing near.

Swift o'er smooth waters they glide,
      As the mist that hangs over the sea;
My chains I will give to the waves,
      And rush to thee, sweet liberty!"

Address to Slavery

By Samuel Wright
The Weekly Anglo-African, February 18, 1860

Slavery, O Slavery! I cannot conceive
Why judges and magistrates do not relieve
My down-trodden people from under thy hand,
Restore them their freedom, and give them their land.

The loud voice of reason incessantly cries,
Ye lovers of Mammon, when will ye be wise?
How long will misanthropy reign in your hearts?
Behold the poor slaves, and consider their smarts.

Upon the plantation they labor and toil,
Exert all their strength to enrichen the soil,
While the sun pours upon them its hot scorching ray,
Without intermission the whole livelong day.

Hope God by His power will save them at last,
And bring them as Israel in ages that's past,
Out of the reach of proud slavery's chain,
To enjoy the sweet comfort of freedom again.

The Sacrifice: 'Up! For It Is Time'

By G. W. Putnam
Douglass' Monthly, November 1860

'Twas eighteen fifty-nine, in cold December,
    'Neath a clear, wintry sky,
The day and hour the world will e'er remember,
    John Brown came forth to die!

With a calm smile he greets the fierce eyes scowling,
    Adown the lengthened line,
And Slavery's ravening wolf pack hush their howling
    Beneath his look divine!

'Whence is this strength? He stands before the scaffold,
    Yet trembles not a limb!'
So asked the tyrants, as with malice baffled
    They wondering gazed on him!

This wise—all night, heeding no sentry's warning.
    Came to his cell that throng;
The same which, in Gethsemane one morning,
    Made a lone spirit strong.

See! from the cliffs which guard the starry regions
    Myriads of eyes look down!
And from the pearly gates pour the bright legions,
    Bearing the martyr's crown!

And hovering near him many a wing of angel
    Gleams in the amber light!
Thou'lt hear, old man, to-day the Christ's evangel,
    And walk with him in white!

He pauses at the gallows' stair—caressing,
    With voice and features mild,
The outcast ones—gives them his latest blessing,
    Kisses the negro child.[5]

Great God! that kiss!—its thrilling hath not perished,
    But on from clime to clime,
Leaping from heart to heart, it shall be cherished
    Till the last pulse of Time!

From the high platform he sees strange lights looming
    Far up the northern sky!
Hears on the wintry breeze the sullen booming
    Of minute guns surge by!

He knows it all!—that a million hearts are bleeding
    In this dark hour for him;
And trembling lips in vast assemblies reading—
    Words that through tears grow dim!

He scans the future with a faith unshaken,
    The Battle he begun—
He knows it stops not—good work well undertaken,
    In due time *must* be done!

---

5   Although factually disputed by historians, many accounts of John Brown's execution record that he paused to kiss an African American child while on his march to the gallows.

His mind on fire with Truth, in its vast reachings
    A deeper law had seen
Than that expressed is the e'er-loving teachings
    Of the good Nazarene.

That deeper LAW OF NATURE, full of beauty!
    The GODHEAD's brightest crown;
JUSTICE TO ALL! and hence the right and duty
    To crush the tyrant down!

For this to-day, beneath the light supernal,
    Thou, mighty one! shalt stand;
And JUSTICE, from the heart of the Eternal,
    Shall bless thy red right hand!

One moment now to fill his glory's measure—
    The silver cord is riven!
The lofty spirit sweeps the sea of azure!
    The martyr is in Heaven!

Bell answers bell; and cannon's voice terrific,
    The boding sounds of woe;
From the Atlantic to the broad Pacific
    Upon the breezes go!

Twice since that day Virginia hath lifted
    Her gibbet, dark and grim,
And there the young, the brave, the true, the gifted,
    Worthily followed him.

And round the rolling world, with deep emotion,
    The Peoples tell the story,
Remembering all their courage and devotion,
    They keep their names in glory!

Nor ends it here—e'en now the night fires glaring
    Light up the robber land;
And houseless tyrants know the Negro's daring,
    And feel his heavy hand!

The cold steel in the twinkling star-light glistens
    Beside the sleeper's bed;
All night the waking mother trembles and listens
    To hear the Avenger's tread!

AND THEY SHALL HEAR IT! e'er the record closes
    That which hath been, shall be
The trampled millions with another Moses
    Shall walk the crimson sea!

Whilst we refine—making the clear yet clearer,
    Prating of Tomes and Laws;
God sleepeth not! but nearer still and nearer
    His fierce circle draws!

The cry that rang so wildly through the Tyrol
    When the *sign* rode the waters!
At its fierce coming, maidens cease your carol,
    Woe! to the South-land's daughters!

The cry of Andrew Hofer[6] through the mountains,
    Shall fill this land of crime!
And cheeks grow pale beside the southern fountains—
    UP NOW! FOR IT IS TIME!

---

6   Andreas Hofer, a Tyrolean patriot who fought for Austria against Napoleon's
    forces during the War of the Third Coalition, led an 1809 rebellion against the
    French that helped spark the War of the Fifth Coalition. Like John Brown, Hofer
    was captured and executed.

John Brown, a radical abolitionist who believed that armed insurrection was the only way to end slavery in the United States, was executed for treason in December 1859 after attempting to seize the U.S. arsenal at Harpers Ferry, Virginia. In October 1859, Brown, accompanied by at least twenty men (including his own sons and several African Americans), raided the arsenal with the intent of seizing weapons and distributing them among slaves for use in rebellion. Although Brown's attempts were thwarted, the raid proved to be one of the major turning points leading to the Civil War: the attack excited many Southerners' fears of slave uprisings, while many Northerners hailed Brown as a hero, martyr, and inspiration to the abolitionist cause.

The Slave Mingo's Poem

*The following remarkable poem was sent on from the South by a
friend, who informs us that the author of it was a slave named
Mingo, a man of wonderful talents and on that grounds oppressed by
his master. While in his slave prison, he penciled this poetic gem on one
of the beams, which was afterwards found and copied. My friend adds
that Mingo did escape, at night, but was recaptured and destroyed by
the bloodhounds. [. . .] The last line was from some cause incomplete;
perhaps his feelings overcame him at the conception. I concluded to
give it as it was found. C. W.*

By Mingo
The Weekly Anglo-African, August 10, 1861

Good God! and must I leave them now—
My wife, my children, in their woe?
'Tis mockery to say I'm sold—
But I forgot these chains so cold,
Which goad my bleeding limbs, though high
My reason mounts above the sky.
Dear wife, they cannot sell the rose
Of love, that in my bosom glows.
Remember, as your tears may start,
They cannot sell th' immortal part;
Thou sun, which lightest bond and free,
Tell me, I pray, is liberty
The lot of those who noblest feel,
And oftest to Jehovah kneel?
Then may I say, but not with pride,
I feel the rushings of the tide
Of reason and of eloquence,

Which strive and yearn for eminence.
I feel high manhood on me now,
A spirit glory on my brow;
I feel a thrill of music roll
Like angel harpings though my soul,
While poesy with rustling wings
Upon my spirit rests and sings.
He sweeps my heart's deep throbbing lyre,
Who touched Isaiah's lips with fire.

To Plymouth Rock, ye breezes bear
These words from me, as I would dare,
If I were free: Is not our God
Our common father? —from the sod
He formed us all! then brothers—yes;
We're brother's all, though some oppress
And grind their equals in the dust,
Oh Heaven! tell me, is this just?
'Tis fiendish. No! I will not go
And leave my children here in woe!
God help me! out, the bright dagger! gleam,
And find the coward's heart, and stream
With fiendish blood—This night, this night,
Or I am free, or shall it shall smite
The master and his slave, and we
Will seek the heavenly liberty!
There will my master's bloody lash
No longer lacerate * * * *

Statue of "The Freed Slave," Memorial Hall Philadelphia; 1876

VOICES BEYOND BONDAGE

Some Hundred Thousands More

The Freedmen's Answer to President Lincoln—1863

Alson Landon Woodward
Western Cyclone, May 17, 1866

We are coming Father Abraham,
      Some hundred thousands more;
We are coming with a gladness,
      That we never felt before.
In the air that laughs with sunshine,
      Something tells us we are free.
There are voices all about us—
      There's a bird in ev'ry tree;
And they tell us, oh they tell us,
      You have said that we might come
From the cotton and the rice fields
      And you'd look us up a home.
With anxiety and trembling,
      For the happiness in store,
We are coming Father Abraham,
      Some hundred thousands more.

We are coming though our freedom
      Has been tarrying so long,
That we almost loved the places
      Of our misery and wrong.
We are bringing for you blessing,
      Such as God alone imparts
Upon those who carry comfort
      Unto trampled human hearts.

From the cane-brakes of Kentucky,
       From the hills of Tennessee;
From the land that rots with treason
       Under Beauregard and Lee:
From the swamps of Carolina,
       And from Alabama's shore,
We are coming father Abraham,
       Some hundred thousands more.

We've been waiting in our cabins;
       We've been looking from the fields
Where the snowy blooming cotton,
       All its rich abundance yields.
For the tidings that should bring us
       What we never yet possessed,
Titles to our wives and children,
       And a right to hope and rest.
Maybe we were singing "Dixie,"
       When "old Massa" went away;
But our hearts were praying wildly
       For the blessing to-day.
"Massas" gone to fight for treason,
       But he left an open door,
And we're coming father Abraham,
       Some hundred thousands more.

We are coming, true and ready,
       To uphold the flag that waves,
Stainless in its starry grandeur,
       Since it flaunts not over slaves.
We've a dark and fearful record,
       Traced in agony and tears;
Yet we only ask for justice,
       In the hopeful future years.

We are coming from the slave pens,
    Where our dear ones have been sold,
Where the sacred name of virtue,
    Has been bartered off for gold.
While God deals with the oppressor,
    Swiftly winnowing His floor,
We are coming Father Abraham
    Some loyal millions more.

While President Lincoln's 1863 Emancipation Proclamation, an executive order, did not abolish slavery, it did demand that all slaves in states in active rebellion be immediately freed and recognized as such by the Union Army. The proclamation did not apply to slaveholding states not in rebellion, nor to states that had already been returned to Union control; legal freedom for slaves in these states awaited the 1865 ratification of the 13th Amendment to the U.S. Constitution. However, the proclamation was a defining moment in history: enslavement of approximately three million human beings immediately ended, and the proclamation was widely regarded as the heralding of freedom for all to follow.

This poem is a takeoff of James Sloan Gibbons's 1862 poem "Three Hundred Thousand More."

Anniversary Poem—July 4, 1867

By J. Willis Ménard [New Orleans, Louisiana]
The New Orleans Tribune, July 7, 1867

Almighty God, enthroned in heaven above;
Dispenser of all good, all peace and love,
Once more we come, and lowly bend the knee,
To thank thee for our new-born liberty!
Through the dark past, 'mid storms and toils of years,
We've watch'd thy coming through our burning tears.
We knew thy coming by the eagle's soar—
The clash of arms and the loud cannon's roar!
Thy quaking earth—the far resounding trees
The nodding mountains and the trembling seas!
And happy now beneath the western sky,
In bonds and fetters we no longer sigh!
For, echoing far beyond the ocean's wave,
The cannon's voice has hush'd the sighing slave.
No more is heard the driver's whip and horn
Resounding through the cotton and the corn:
The slave-hounds in the swamp no longer bark,
The slave no longer travels in the dark,
But in great freedom's light, of recent birth,
He walks erect, a sovereign of the earth!
The coming day of which the prophets told,
Now gilds the western horizon with gold;
Presaging evermore the reign of Right,
And the eternal death of wrong and might!
Triumphant let the hosts of freedom tread
Down in the dust foul treason's hydra head;

Let them dethrone the vulgar President[7]
And make him with his rebel hordes repent!
For truly he has made freedom a sham,
Since the sad death of father Abraham;
Rewarding traitors with unending fame
And bowing the head of loyalty in shame.
Ah! had the nation's fallen chief[8] survived,
The traitor-chief[9] on gallows would have died:
Treason would have been made a heinous crime,
And traitors punished all through coming time.
Ah! had he lived, poor Afric's driven race,
Would have no cause to sue for rebel grace;
For o'er this wide extended southern land,
Justice and loyalty would now command.
But let us trust the justice of our laws,
Congress has met again to raise our cause![10]
And soon will the brave millions, black and white,
Hurl treason and rebels from their height!
Oh! then shall peace and happiness have come,
When loyalty shall rule in every home:
When man, regardless of his hue, shall find
A common brotherhood in all mankind;
Where there shall be as far as men have trod,
One common right—one liberty—one God!
Then onward let us march in freedom's van!
With Grant and Butler, Pope and Sheridan!
Let it be known wherever man have trod,
The voice of freemen is the voice of God!

---

7   Andrew Johnson, 17th president of the Unites States.
8   Abraham Lincoln, 16th president of the United States.
9   Jefferson Davis, president of the Confederate States of America.
10 The 14th Amendment to the U.S. Constitution, which ensured citizenship and
    equal protection under the law to all males, was making its way through Congress
    when this poem was published.

Following the 1865 assassination of Abraham Lincoln, Vice President Andrew Johnson—a pro-Union Democrat from Tennessee—assumed the presidency. Johnson was no friend to Republicans and/or African Americans: he twice vetoed the Civil Rights Act of 1866; opposed the 14th Amendment to the U.S. Constitution; and implemented a Presidential Reconstruction plan that was far more sympathetic to former secessionist states than many Republicans preferred. In this poem, Menard, a radical Republican, argues that African American civil rights would have been secured without the intervention of Congress if Lincoln had lived and that Lincoln would have severely punished Confederate officers and leaders.

II

Dedications &
Remembrances

On Viewing the Lifeless Remains
of a Very Dear Friend

By Louisa
Freedom's Journal, December 7, 1827

Oh! thine was love so pure and sweet,
    So tender, firm, and so sincere,
How often have we met to greet
    Each new, each happy year.

Then hours flew unheeded by,
    With giddy mirth and song:
But death, alas! has clos'd thy eye,
    Which shone in pleasure's throng.

But now how changed those happy days;
    How alter'd now is every scene!
There all I lov'd in silence lays,
    Calmly as if she ne'er had been.

Yes, thou art gone! and with thee fled
    All sense of pain, or fears;
Silent, reposing with the dead,
    Unconscious of our tears.

Lines on the Death of
Reverend Jeremiah Gloucester

By Amicus
Freedom's Journal, January 25, 1828

Is Gloucester dead! The man of God?
Why! I saw him, but the other day
With cheerfulness upon his brow,
Oh! has he now so soon decayed!

Yes, I saw him, mount the sacred desk;
There, with energy proclaim the truth,
While, listening ears, hung upon his lips;
And is it possible, he's dead and gone!

What, gone—left his newly wedded bride—
Forlorn, to weep and mourn—a widow!
Left the people of his charge alone?
Has he gone and left the world forever!

Depart'd, in the morning of his days,
In the blooming primrose of life;
'Mid, the hope of future usefulness;
Is he suddenly cut down—by death!

Yes, I read the record of his death!—
While I read, my bosom palpitates;
Tender tears come rushing to my eyes;
But, oh, delightful cheering thought; that,

THOUGH he moulders in his silent URN,
He's free from every care and pain;
Gone to rest from all this labours here;
And to receive a *rich reward* in HEAVEN!

*Jeremiah Gloucester (1799–1827) was pastor of the Second African Presby-
terian Church in Philadelphia. He was born into slavery. His father John,
after attaining his own freedom, raised funds to free his wife and four children
and settled the family in Philadelphia, where he became pastor of the First
African Presbyterian Church. Jeremiah followed his father's footsteps into
the ministry and in 1824 became pastor of the Second Church.*

Our Sister

By Mrs. M. Christain [Boston, Massachusetts]
Mirror of Liberty, March 1839

Sister Jennie thou have left us,
    Here thy loss we deeply feel;
But 'tis God that has bereft us,
    He can all our sorrows heal.

Weep no more for her, dear mother,
    She has reached that blest abode,
In the house of our dear Saviour,
    King of Kings and Lord of Lords.

Weep no more for her, dear sister;
    She has broke the ice and gone,
With the banner of King Jesus,
    Stained with the Saviour's precious blood.

Let us then march boldly onward,
    Till we reach the Shining Shore,
There we'll see our Blessed Saviour;
    There we'll meet to part no more.

The Palladium of Liberty

BY G. W. ROOTS
The Palladium of Liberty, December 27, 1843

It is in eighteen hundred and forty three,
When we present the Palladium of Liberty;
It was not got up on speculation,
But to 'meliorate the colored people's condition.

This paper has been presented to us
By the colored people of Columbus,
We hope to delineate the chains of slavery
By the force of the Palladium of Liberty.

Then we will praise Jehovah's name,
That we the Africans are proclaiming,
That we will not be held enslaved
By barbarous minds of men enraged.

We'll not see the enslav'd mother mourn—
Her children from her bosom torn.
We'll not see them dragg'd into slavery,
In all the scenes of agony.

*This poem was penned in celebration of the
inaugural issue of* The Palladium of Liberty,
*which was founded by David Jenkins and
"devoted to the interests of colored people generally." The short-lived Ohio
paper offered strong editorial support on issues such as abolition, education
of African American children, temperance, and moral reform.*

David Jenkins

Memory of Clarkson

Lines Occasioned by the Death
of the Great and Good Thomas Clarkson

By Anonymous
The North Star, January 7, 1848

Clarkson! revered in every clime
Where Mercy lifts her voice sublime,
Immortal honors—guiltless fame—
Deep in our hearts have set thy name.

The patriot's wreath, though bright, must fade;
The diadem, by mortals made,
Grows dim and pale, beside that crown
Which circles thy unsought renown.

Thy simple majesty of mind,
Thy lofty purpose, well defined,
Shall stand before that searching eye
Which every motive can descry.

A foreign shore, the stranger's land,
The pathless waste, the burning sand,
Witnessed alike thy steady aim
A nation's sorrows to proclaim.

To break the fetters of the slave
Thy great resolve had aimed to save,
And change them to that golden chain,
By Heaven designed, from Heaven which came:

The links composed, since time began,
Of boundless love to erring man,
Though dimmed awhile and blended here
With strange alloy of guilt and fear.

Illustrious hero, great and good,
No trophies, stained with human blood,
Above thy honored dust shall wave,
To mock thy pure, unblemished grave.

Friend of my race, farewell! farewell!
Affection weeps to hear thy knell;
Thy requiem shall be fondly sung,
In distant land and foreign tongue.

And when thou standest at "the gate,"
Where countless myriads trembling wait,
Thine be the great reward to win—
"My faithful servant, enter in!"

Thomas Clarkson (1760–1846) was arguably Great Britain's greatest leader of the transatlantic abolitionist moment. He was a founding member of the Society for Effecting the Abolition of the Slave Trade (1787) and was instrumental in the passing of the Slave Trade Act of 1807, which abolished the British transatlantic slave trade. In 1823, he also helped found the Society for the Mitigation and Gradual Abolition of Slavery Throughout the British Dominions. In the latter years of his career, he campaigned against slavery throughout Europe and America, serving as the keynote speaker of the inaugural 1840 World Anti-Slavery Convention. His efforts are remembered by Americans and the British alike; William Wordsworth penned a sonnet to Clarkson and several memorials have been erected to his memory.

Forget Me Not

"Thou'lt forget me when I'm gone." —Shakespeare

By J. P.
The North Star, February 18, 1848

Forget thee! ah! and canst thou think
  Affection's bonds so cold,
That blighting time soon rusts the link
  Which bound the heart of old?
Though the kindled flame may paler grow,
  Because it is not fed,
The vital spark still grows below,
  Till life within is fled.

Forget thee! no! when pleasure fills
  Her goblets to the brim,
And mirth and joy, like sparkling rills,
  No breath of care may dim;
When sorrow's clouds are gathered round
  The heart that once was gay;
When the somber veil of night is bound
  Around the face of day.

Forget thee! no! while fancy moulds
  Bright images that last,
While the sleepless eye of memory holds
  Its vigils o'er the past.
Forget thee! no! when death is near,
  To claim the tribute due,
One constant thought shall draw the tear—
  That thought so full of you.

The Star and the Child

By Anonymous
The North Star, March 9, 1849

A maiden walked at eventide,
    Beside a clear and placid stream,
And smiled, as in its depths she saw
    A trembling star's reflected beam.

She smiled until the beam was lost,
    As 'cross the sky a cloud was driven,
And then she sighed, and then forgot
    The star was shining still in heaven.

A mother sat beside life's stream,
    Watching a dying child at dawn,
And smiled, as in its eye she saw
    A hope that it might still live on.

She smiled until the eyelids closed,
    But watched for breath until the even;
And then she wept, and then forgot
    The child was living still in heaven.

My Pen

By Frank Addison Mowig Philom [Rochester, New York]
Frederick Douglass' Paper, February 5, 1852

My pen, my pen, my joy and my pride,
My idol I worship each day;
A gem which adversity giveth to me,
Shall speak of the shackles, the bond and the free,
And sound thy loud anthems o'er woodland and lea,
To echo forever and aye.

My pen, my pen, thou hope of my youth,
What visions I saw in thy name;
My castles have fallen, alas! I am left,
From friends and from kindred, and almost bereft,
I feel the cold pinions around me are pressed
That shall stifle my infant-like frame.

My pen, my pen, I wished not for thee
To leave me a gainer of gold,
No—motives more pure, I trust now impart
A halo of love still nearer my heart,
That shall shine with more brilliance when lucre and art
Are with the past ages enrolled.

My pen, my pen, thou noblest of arms,
Thou "Grand Worthy Scribe" of the world,
'Tis not for thy name, but thy valueless worth,
That maketh thee my dearest of treasures on earth,
And calls for loud praises round each peasant's hearth,

Where beauty's so clearly unfurled.

My pen, my pen, there is joy in thy name.
My heart shall be ever thine own;
While a Washington's banner round us shall wave,
Oh! stretch forth thy hand like an angel to save
From deep tears of anguish a FREE COUNTRY'S SLAVE,
That *the stain* be forever unknown.

My pen, my pen, when I leave this dark sphere,
And pass to another more blest,
'Tis now my fond wish that there I may be
Engaged in recording some virtues of thee,
Who hast in thy might caused the SLAVE to stand free,
And at last reach a haven of rest.

To *****

By H. E. G. D.
Frederick Douglass' Paper, February 12, 1852

Incarnate Truth and Right, for paltry gold,
The damned Iscariot to the smiters sold:
But lo! the bribe, hotter than coals from hell,
Burns on the conscience of the Infidel,
And Hates and Horrors darken o'er his sky,
And fierce Remorse, wild Fear, and dark Despair,
Fill with foul fiends the suffocating air,
Till every breath he draws is torture's pang,
And every fiber is the demon's fang.

For paltry gold hast *thou*, with bloodhound zeal,
Hunted the poor, and crushed them 'neath thy heel;
With deep-bayed vengeance howl'd upon their track:
To Slavery's hell intent to drag them back;
Plundered the weak and driven them to roam
Far from the shelter of a peaceful home;
And, like a Herod, smitten with the rod
Of godless power the ministers of God!

Exult, oh Fool! to see thy coffers swell
With heaped-up gold—thy price for serving hell!
And when, before the sacramental board
Thou standst, *professed* disciple of the Lord,
Then think of JUDAS, and his strength be thine
To take and taste the consecrated wine:
Nor fear that Conscience will destroy its least—

Conscience, with Honor, has been laid to rest.

What though, like Judas, thou hast not the grace
To take the *same* conveyance to "his place?"
The longer route, perhaps, thy turn may serve,
Besides, this hanging needs a steady nerve,
And tremulous hands might bungle at the rope,
And make us sick with long-deferred hope.

> *The author compares the addressee of this poem to Judas Iscariot, the apostle who—according to Christian tradition—"sold" Jesus to the High Priest Caiaphas, who then turned Jesus over to the Romans for crucifixion. Most traditions hold that Judas, in anguish and regret, later hung himself.*
>
> *While the author identifies neither himself/herself nor the person to whom this poem is addressed, judging from the date and context the "******" of the title is most likely President Fillmore or prominent Democratic Senator Stephen A. Douglas, both of whom were instrumental in passing the 1850 Fugitive Slave Act. Also known as the "Bloodhound Law," the act required that escaped slaves caught in free states be returned to their masters. (See also "To Mr. Fillmore" and "The Rescue of Jerry.")*

The Moral Hero

Suggested by the late Speech in Congress of Mr. Giddings.

BY ANONYMOUS
Frederick Douglass' Paper, October 15, 1852

The thirst of fame inspires the soul-lit page,
      And bids the canvass glow, the marble breathe;
      O, immorality! thy burning wreath
Hath lured the human soul through every age!
Nor vain the hope, even in this earthly stage;
      Nor aught, even here, save virtue, gives the crown!
      'Twas twined for Phocion, Cato, 'neath the frown
Of fortune, and the fickle people's rage,
And brighter blooms while sculpture falls to dust:
      Even thus, O GIDDINGS! shall it deck thy brow,
While all earth's marble piles betray their trust:
      Yon "Modern Capitol" to time must bow—
But bravely, sternly, "obstinately just,"
      A victor of the immortal heights are thou!

*Joshua R. Giddings, Republican of Ohio, served in the U.S. House of Repre-
sentatives 1838–59 and was a fierce opponent of slavery. He was a founding
member of the Republican party and introduced scores of anti-slavery bills
during his time in office. (See "To Joshua R. Giddings" and "Southrons.")*

To Mr. Fillmore

On His Retirement from the Presidency

By Q.
Frederick Douglass' Paper, March 18, 1853

Oh, Mr. Millard Fillmore!
    Your hour of pride is past;
The string is broken of your kite,
    And down it comes at last.
Your accidental honors
    Are like a vision fled;
The nation saw your lack of brains,
    And got another head!

Oh, wondrous Mr. Fillmore!
    You're ranked among the great:
The reason doubtless is, you weigh
    About two hundred weight.
This sort of greatness ought to be
    A caution, I should think;
Because the greater some folks are,
    The sooner will they sink.

Oh, patriotic Fillmore!
    Should History of you tell,
She'll say you loved your country
    "Not wisely, but too well."
A hundred thousand men-thieves
    To you appeared as good

Suspected fugitives being hunted under the terms
of the Fugitive Slave Law; 1850

As Twenty Million honest folks
 Who earn their livelihood.

Oh, pious Mr. Fillmore!
 You doubtless sing and pray;
You read your Bible, go to church,
 And keep the Sabbath-day,
And yet you aid in catching slaves[11]
 (Oppression's hateful tool!)
And punish men, by fine and jail,
 Who keep the Golden Rule.

Oh, hopeful Mr. Fillmore!
 I sometimes wonder how

---

11 References the 1850 Fugitive Slave Act.

Your children's sons will think of you,
    Say fifty years from now.
Dear Filly, we should ne'er forget
    That Truth alone endures;
And Cain and Judas then may have
    As good repute as yours.

Oh, Mr. Millard Fillmore!
    Your native Empire State
Will doubtless think a deal of you,
    So pious, good and great.
Fair Gotham's streets and Erie's shore
    Will not forget your name,
And all the Jerry Rescuers[12]
    Shall help you on to fame.

Millard Fillmore, the thirteenth U.S. president, 1850–53, assumed the office following Zachary Taylor's death in July 1850. Fillmore signed into law the Fugitive Slave Act of 1850 (aka, the "Bloodhound Law"), which required that fugitive slaves caught living in free states (or territories) be returned to their masters.

---

12 See note in "The Rescue of Jerry."

The Beggar Girl

By ETHIOP [Brooklyn, New York]
Frederick Douglass' Paper, March 17, 1854

As I went from home one wintry morning,
The winds were fierce, and it was storming,
A little stranger, wan and wild,
Cried, Give! Oh, give a needy child!

I, without grudging, without hoarding,
Gave what ere my purse affording—
Received in turn a mournful smile,
'Twas the thanks of a *beggar child.*

I, soon amidst the business moving,
Buying, selling, praising, proving,
As is the custom of the world,
Forgot the little *beggar girl.*

At night, I sat by my fire, weary;
All without was dreary, dreary;
The bleak winds in a fearful whirl,
And then recurred the *beggar girl.*

Fond sleep and heavy eyes refusing,
I fell into a solemn musing,
Over the coldness of the world,
And trials of the *beggar girl.*

My thoughts still onward, onward fleeting,
Sorrows, suffering, buffets meeting,
In their swift flight round the world,
They'd meet anon the *beggar girl.*

As deeper in my revery falling,
Lo! a voice seemed to me calling,
Oh! oh! is this a friendless world?
'Twas like the little *beggar girl.*

Though yet into my revery seeming,
Now in truth was dreaming—dreaming
About the cold and heartless world,
And dream'd I saw the *beggar girl.*

Next morn, beneath my window lonely,
Went a horse and driver only,
Unnoticed by the world—
They said it bore the *beggar girl.*

When wintry winds my cot is rocking,
And storm at my door is knocking,
I then reflect upon the world,
And ne'er forget the *beggar girl.*

> *Although the content of this poem is entirely original, these verses are loosely modeled after Edgar Allan Poe's 1845 poem,* The Raven.

Whipping in North Carolina; 1867

VOICES BEYOND BONDAGE

Southrons

By Daniel Haynes [East Nassau, New York]
Frederick Douglass' Paper, June 30, 1854

So chivalrous Southrons, you've triumph'd again,
And added more links to the long "coffle chain".
Curtailed the dominion of generous freedom,
And prepared future markets for slaves, as you breed 'em.
Your bloody slave-banner you've widely unfurl'd,
And rendered your country the scorn of the world;
You are fondly expecting at some future day,
Where now the wild beasts and the savages stay,
To see broad plantations of that fertile soil
Enriched!—no, exhausted, by sweat, blood and toil—
Extorted from slaves by the o'erseer's lash—
No matter, provided you get but the cash.
You see in prospective the slave trader come,
The dread of the slave in his Kentucky home,
For Nebraska's new market a gang to obtain—
Slave-trader, slave-breeder, both traffic for gain;
What cares he or you for the poor negro's pain?
Slave pens, chains and handcuffs are in requisition,
And bargains are struck with specific condition;
The wife and the husband are torn from each other,
The mother from children—the children from mother.
What reeks either buyer or seller these rigors?
No matter whatever, they are nothing but niggers,
Arranged in due order, attached to the chain,
For Nebraska they're bound, to be sold once again.
Arrived at that market, no doubt you may see

That Tom, Dick and Harry are sold to Legree,[13]
While Nancy and Emma, and Betty, so fair,
With skin nearly white, and their long narrow hair,
To lecherous bachelors, buried in vice,
Are sold at a very exorbitant price.
No doubt you're rejoicing in anticipation
Of seeing that spacious domain of the nation,
On which you've so lately a charter bestowed,
Subjected to slavery's most damnable code,
And peopled with slaves of each varying shade,
From black man and woman, to white boy and maid.
Thousands such you may number by tens and by twelves,
Though born of slave mothers, begot by yourselves.
You often declare in imperious tone
That 'tis nothing to us, for the slaves are our own;
And so truly are they, beyond misconstruction,
Your title being founded upon reproduction.
Who, then, shall forbid you to keep or to hold,
Or sell your own children for bright, shining gold?
Though people may utter some adverse suggestions,
Just say, they're my own, and that answers all questions;
But Southrons, I spare you, nor would be unkind,
Long habit to justice has rendered you blind:
You see not the evils amid which you live,
So your conduct I'm half-way disposed to forgive;
. But what shall I say to that recreant band
Of men, born and reared on that part of our land
Where no slave is e'er seen, unless it may be
Some fugitive seeking in vain to be free?
Ye Judases, Esaus, your birth right you've sold!

---

13 Hayes is alluding to *Uncle Tom's Cabin* by Harriet Beecher Stowe. Simon Legree
    is Tom's cruelest owner, who eventually orders him whipped to death. By 1854,
    only two years after the publication of Stowe's work, the name Legree had become
    synonymous with cruelty and greed.

VOICES BEYOND BONDAGE

But no mess of pottage, nor silver, nor gold,
Will you ever obtain; for your purchasers know
That no favor on you will the people bestow.
From shame and derision, reproach and contempt,
Henceforth and forever you'll ne'er be exempt.
Go, prostrate yourselves, ye base miscreants, knaves;
Go, prostrate yourselves to the masters of slaves,
And there plead the service you've rendered their cause,
By enacting their slave territorial laws.
Think you they'll reward you? Their boots you may lick,
And perhaps for your pains they may give you a kick;
Full well, ye deserve it, 'tis justly your due,
So meekly receive it, ye groveling crew.
Disgusted and loathing, I leave you to roll
In moral putrescency, body and soul.
For the muse now invites to a worthier day,
And bids tune the lyre, a just tribute to pay,
To that noble squadron of patriots good,
Who, although outnumbered, yet firmly withstood
That hell-hatch'd concoction of falsehood and fraud,
Injurious to man, and offensive to God.
All hail to you, champions of Freedom and Right,
Whom bribes cannot purchase, nor threatenings fright.
Like Milton's Abdiel,[14] who, although alone,
Durst resist Satan's treason 'gainst God's holy throne.
So Caleb and Joshua once stood arrayed
Against thirty-eight cowards of giants afraid.
There were giants in Canaan, 'tis very well known,
And we have one giant[15] at least of our own.
Those giants of Canaan caused cowards to quail,

---

14 A heavenly being in *Paradise Lost*.
15 Refers to Stephen A. Douglas, U.S. Senator (1847–61). Known as the Senate's
   "Little Giant," Douglas was short in stature but a powerful political leader. He
   vehemently worked to push the 1850 Fugitive Slave Act through Congress.

Our giant caused Senators' courage to fail;
But you stood undaunted in Truth's holy cause,
Opposing that base-born reproach of all laws
That legalized slavery, with all its array
Of plagues, such as Egypt ne'er saw in her day;
While down time's long current your names shall descend,
When each son shall boast that his sire was your friend:
Everlasting remembrance shall be your blest lot,
While the names of your foes and oppressors shall rot.
O! had I the pow'rs of a Milton or Young,
Or of the Apostles, the manifold tongue,
To all present nations your worth I'd proclaim,
And all future ages should echo your fame.

See notes at "'Tis the Worst and the Best" and "Nebraska and Slavery."

To Frederick Douglass

Written after hearing him lecture.

By R. [Jamestown, New York]
Frederick Douglass' Paper, October 13, 1854

Go forth! thou noble patriot, go,
      And plead for Freedom through the land;
Our country's baseness boldly shows,
      Though myriads now the truth withstand.

Go! speak of Cruelty and Wrong,
      Which millions of our race endure;
Be ever valiant, faithful, strong,
      Engaged in such a mission pure.

Such eloquence is seldom known,
      As that, untaught, thou canst command;
Scholastic art men freely own,
      Before it is a rope of sand.

Would that I could like thee portray,
      The matchless garb which Freedom wears;
No—no—tell how 'twas snatched away,
      And left humanity in tears.

When future years shall roll away;
      And Liberty once more shall reign,
A thousand tongues that scoff to-day,
      Will shout their praises to thy name.

And when at last thy labors here,
      Are brought triumphant to a close,
Heaven's messengers shall come to cheer,
      As through Death's vale thy spirit goes.

To Joshua R. Giddings

On consenting to become a Candidate for Congress.

By K. L. C [South Grove, Illinois]
Frederick Douglass' Paper, October 27, 1854

Go on, brave man!
And lead the van,
As long thou hast in Freedom's cause,
At thy stern voice,
Freemen rejoice,
And tyrants tremble when they pause.

With thy vast might,
Maintain the right,
And all the bondman's wrongs disclose;
For thou canst save
The down-cast slave,
Or *more* can check his tide of woes.

In Congress Hall
Roll Freedom's ball
Through the array of whips and chains:
And by good laws,
Promote the cause,
Of Justice on Columbia's plains.

In that lion's den,
Thy speech and pen
Have given tyrants first alarm;
And drawn from the North

Of the frantic South,
Not the right to save, but the power to harm.

The rights of all
White, black, great, small,
And cheerfully dost thou defend,
And thus men see,
Centered in thee,
Best proofs of an impartial friend.

Our country calls,
And Freedom's halls
Cannot dispense with thy great power;
No private shade
Was ever made
For patriots in a trial hour.

Then let us pray,
God speed the day,
When tyranny its course has run;
And every trace
Of the pirate race
Be blotted out beneath the sun.

See earlier note about Giddings at "The Moral Hero."

The Dead Soldier

Lines on a soldier found lying dead on the field of battle.

By Anonymous
Frederick Douglass' Paper, February 2, 1855

Wreck of a warrior passed away!
  Thou form without a name!
Which thought and felt but yesterday,
  And dreamt of future fame,—
Stripped of thy garments, who shall guess
Thy rank, thy lineage, and race?
If haughty chieftain, holding sway,
Or lowlier, destined to obey?

The light of that fixed eye is set,
  And all is moveless now,
But Passion's traces linger yet,
  And lower upon that brow;
Expression has not yet waxed weak,
The lips seem e'en to speak,
And clenched the old and lifeless hand,
As if it grasped the battle brand!

Though from that head, late towering high,
  The waving plume is torn,
And low in dust that form doth lie,
  Dishonored and forlorn;
Yet death's dark shadow cannot hide
The graven characters of pride,
That on the lip and brow reveal

The impress of the spirit's seal.

Lives there a mother, to deplore
   The son she ne'er shall see?
Or maiden on some distant shore,
   To break her heart for thee?
Perchance to roam a maniac there,
With wild-flower wreaths to deck her hair,
And through the weary night to wait
Thy footstep at the lonely gate.

Long shall she linger there, in vain
   The evening fire shall trim,
And, gazing on the darkening main,
   Shall often call on him
Who hears her not—who cannot hear.
Oh! deaf forever is the ear
That once in listening rapture hung
Upon the music of her tongue!

Long may she dream,—to wake is woe!
   Ne'er may remembrance tell
Its tale, to bid her sorrows flow,
   And hope to sigh farewell;
The heart, bereaving of its stay,
Quenching the beam that cheers her way
Along the waste of life,—till she
Shall lay her down, and sleep like thee!

My Friend

By Jenny Marsh [Rochester, New York]
Frederick Douglass' Paper, June 8, 1855

I do not weep for thee,
    Loved one and lost,
Casting wild murmurs on my lot God-given,
    And dear hopes crost,
And frowning back the smile that won to heaven
    The one loved most.

'Tis very true I never cease to miss thee,
    Though glad hearts 'round me throng,
Though love-warm lips in friendship's troth do kiss me,
And happier days than these do softly wish me,
    Yet I am all alone,
With an unbroken silence in my heart,
    A silence ever cold,
Unless fond memories of thee do start
From sacred biers, and flit across my heart
    With precious words of old.

Yet weep I not thee,
    Loved one so dear,
When as thy chosen friend I stood
    Beside thy bier.
Full well I know with crushing, clinging pain,
Thy folded hands would ne'er clasp mine again,
Nor charm the throbbing from my aching brow,
And break the shadows resting there e'en now.

I watch the buds that blossom on thy bed,
        Frail, fading things like me,
But rather mark the stars above my head,
Each one an angel guard above thy bed,—
And while I gaze, my yearnings are half fled,
        They are so like to thee,—
            Far up and very bright,
        But very far from me.

How can I weep for thee,
        Loved one at rest,
And wish thee here again,
And toiling on in pain
        With thorns deep in my breast?
I love thee all too well, loved one, so blest.

And if my tears do fall,
        'Tis not for thee, sweet friend;
'Tis but the struggle of my weary soul,
With yearnings that meek peace may not control,
        That this long way might end,
And my torn feet pause at the golden gates,
        When thou dost wait, my friend,
Still wearing the love-chain that binds our souls,
        The chain death could not rend.

Not Fully Identified

By Miss Martha T. Poor
The Weekly Anglo-African, March 24, 1860

"Not fully known!" Oh, friends who gather round her,
    Amid the anguish of this hour of fear,
Through all the horrors of the fate that bound her,
    Was this the form that ye have held so dear?

Lover, within whose ear a voice still lingers,
    Thrilling thy soul as words may never tell,
Canst thou not say, were these the trembling fingers
    Whose lightest touch thy heart has loved so well?

Mother, who bore and nursed the tender flower,
    Shielding her close from aught like rude alarms,
Canst thou not tell if, in an evil hour,
    Was this the child who left thy sheltering arms?

Father, who saw the light of thy dark dwelling
    Fade slowly out when she had left thy side,
Canst thou not know, amidst thy tears fast swelling,
    Was this the daughter of thy love and pride?

Sister, thou knowest who at morn and even
    Breathed the same prayer at the fond mother's knee—
Listened to the same sweet words of hope and heaven—
    Come, look upon her now; can this be she?

Brother, who, with a fond, protecting duty,
　　　Treasured the sister in thine eyes so fair,
Come, look upon this wreck of what was beauty—
　　　Thou surely canst not claim her lying there!

Ah! there is One who knows—to whose clear seeing
　　　All this dark hour is bright with infinite truth;
Trust Him in faith; the treasures of our being
　　　He will give back to an immortal youth.

Not here—not now—even to our passionate grieving;
　　　But when we stand with her before His throne,
All that to us seems dark and past believing,
　　　Shall, in the clearer light, be "fully known."

The Cry of the Loser

By R. J. Chiles
The Weekly Anglo-African, April 27, 1861

Farewell, the time has come, and we must part,
 Though hearts throb quick and bitter teardrops start,
And the lips quiver to be kissed again,
 And the sweet eyes grow dim and full of pain.

After tonight the face of all life changes,
 The sweet face of the future once so bright,
This sudden rush of clouds all hope estranges;
 Nothing will seem the same after to-night.

The roots of this deep love through all my being
 Run thick as veins; in ev'ry fibre twine;
There is no face on earth to me worth seeing,
 Death coveted, so sweet, so dear as thine.

Death is a door at which we fain would pause
 Long ere we knock. And so dear love did I
Strive to ward off the chill of its dread laws,
 By the warm fires of thy lip and eye.

Farewell, 'tis thus the heart gives up the things,
 That makes existence pleasant. Thus death's knife,
Severs the vine that round our being clings,
 And cuts away the sweetest part of life.

Rest O beloved, no more shalt thou toss,
    Upon life's deep, or hear its winds arise;
Nor strain thy gaze through night to see across,
    The moaning waves, the flush of Paradise.

Studio portrait of Jack & Abby; circa 1875

The Old Man to His Wife

By Anonymous
The Christian Recorder, January 17, 1863

You say the're wrinkles in your face,
  But I can see none there.
Oh! why should Time his record trace
  Upon a page so fair?
You call them wrinkles, love, but still,
  In *this* we don't agree;
For you may call them what you will,
  They *dimples* seem to me.

That youth doth swiftly speed away,
  Has oft been said and sung:
Ah, me! It seems but yesterday
  Since you and I were young;
Then, graceful was your youthful head,
  With glossy, dark brown hair;
You say there's many a silver thread,
  Old Time has woven there.

Well, well! what matter, dark or gray,
  Or smooth or wrinkled brow?
Thou wert not in thy palmiest day
  More beautiful than now;
For still is thine the winning grace,
  The gentle spirit thine,
That sheds o'er young or aged face
  A loveliness divine.

The Slave to His Star

By William Slade [Washington, D.C.]
The Weekly Anglo-African, September 19, 1863

Bright star, of all stars beloved,
    To thee I turned from dreams erewhile;
Far up in God's free heaven unmoved,
    I saw by night thy ceaseless smile,
Lighting a path of hope afar,
    Freedom's high watchfire for the free—
Steadfast and solitary star,
    I felt that fire was lit for me!

I gaze upon thy Northern light,
    That never fails, and falters never,
But hang far over day and night,
    From Heaven's wall shine down forever;
I seem to hear a voice of God
    Speak through the silence down to me,
"Thy feet are strong, thy way is broad,
    The star shall be my path for thee."

Hiding in darkling caves by day,
    With toiling footsteps through the night,
To me came down thy guardian ray,
    A burning lamp, a shining light!
The Red Sea of my pilgrim road,
    Whose parted waves hung threateningly,
I traversed while that beacon glowed,
    And freedom's fettered slave is free.

Star of the slave, crown of the free,
      The eternal midnight's dearest gem,
My race from midnight look to thee,
      As Bethlehem's star art thou to them.
Forever dear their light above,
      Their path below through wood and wave,
Their evening star of trust and love,
      Thou pilot of pathless slave!

Under the Snow

By Anonymous
The Christian Recorder, March 4, 1865

Under the Snow our baby lies,
The fringed lids dropped o'er her eyes;
The tiny hands upon her breast,
Like twin-born lilies taking rest;
While o'er her grave the rough winds blow;
Under the snow—under the snow.

Under the snow our baby lies,
While we sit at home and list for her cries;
And her mother asks, (she is very lone,)
"Why has my little baby gone?"
Ah! happy she feeleth not our woe;
Under the snow—under the snow.

Under the snow our baby lies,
As pure as the clouds far up in the skies—
Those delicate banners of vapor, furled
Beyond the breath of this noisome world.
'Tis the blood of Christ hath made her so;
Under the snow—under the snow.

Above the snow our baby dwells,
Where never the solemn death-bell knells;
Where Sin and Death are never known,
Nor dark-browed Pain, with her voice of moan;
Where the angels move on wings that glow;

Above the snow—above the snow.

Above the snow our baby dwells,
And we dry our tears when we think she swells
The song of the angels and just men there,
With a voice so sweet, and a face so fair.
And we're glad we've sent them a voice from below;
Above the snow—above the snow.

In Memory of Abraham Lincoln

By Anonymous [Palmetto, Louisiana]
The New Orleans Tribune, August 20, 1865

There is no nook nor corner
Upon this mighty sphere,
But that some patriot mourner
Is bowed in fervent prayer,
For him who is departed,
The just, the true, the brave,
The fearless loyal-hearted,
The friend of the friendless slave.
Thy name, O chief immortal,
Shall live as long as time,
Inscribed o'er every portal,
In every land and clime;
And when thy name resound,
Be it to stand or fall,
The black man shall be found
Responsive to the call.
Freedom's works are stronger;
No foe can bridge the stream;
The nation's life is longer,
Its death was but a dream.

This poem was published a mere four months after the assassination of President Abraham Lincoln, when much of the nation was still in mourning.

Most Respectfully Dedicated to the 73D,
Late First Regiment Louisiana Native Guards

By ANONYMOUS [Palmetto, Louisiana]
The New Orleans Tribune, September 5, 1865

Welcome ye sable heroes!
With swords and bayonets bright;
Plumed in war's regalias—
Ye victors of the fight.
Then welcome home, ye gallant boys,
Ye sable boys in blue,
With bayonets bright,
You've won the fight.
We gladly welcome you.

What though the flag be tattered,
Fling it to the breeze.
What though your ranks are shattered,
They tell of victories.
Thrice welcome home, ye gallant boys,
Ye sable boys in blue.
Right shoulders swift with bayonets bright,
We gladly welcome you.

Port Hudson's blood-stained hills,
And labyrinthine bayous,
And brooks and streams and murmuring rills,

All wait the brave Cailloux.[16]
Then welcome home, ye gallant boys,
Ye sable boys in blue.
Charge left, charge right,
We gladly welcome you.

The brazen guns are muzzled now,
The bugle blasts no more.
In the distant sky the promised bow
Of peace is bending o'er.
Thrice welcome home, ye gallant boys,
Ye sable boys in blue.
With bayonets bright,
You've won the fight;
We gladly welcome you.

> The 1st Louisiana Native Guard, based in Union-controlled New Orleans, was the first African American regiment to fight in combat during the Civil War. In late May 1863 the 1st Guard laid siege against the nearby town of Port Hudson, a Confederate stronghold and important gateway to Mississippi river access. Although the 1st Guard was ultimately unable to hold Port Hudson, the port was soon surrendered to the Union following the fall of Vicksburg.

---

16 André Cailloux, captain of the 1st Louisiana Native Guard, was one of the first Americans of African descent to hold an officer's commission in the Union Army. He is remembered for his gallantry during the fighting at Port Hudson, where he lost his life in service.

A Welcome to Major Gen. N. P. Banks

On His Return to New Orleans, 1865

BY A. CITIZEN
The American Citizen, April 19, 1879

Welcome nature's gifted son, the statesman and the hero,
The man that would not welcome him, his soul must be at zero;
Ye men of toil throughout the earth, you owe a debt of thanks
Unto our statesman hero, Nathaniel Prentiss Banks.

Welcome from your Northern clime, New England well may boast,
Her statesmen, poets, heroes, a great and goodly host.
Webster, Everett, Sumner, soar high in historic ranks,
But deeply in the National heart is Major Gen. Banks.

Welcome to your Southern home, right welcome shall you be,
Where you have labored long and well, to make our country free;
We bless the day that brought you here, Louisiana to reclaim,
May laurels thickly on you fall to crown your glorious name.

Welcome to the conqueror, Port Hudson's[17] deeds will shine,
And blazon down the vista of everlasting time,
Not like the deeds of vassaled Rome, or even ancient Greece,
Our conquest are not slaves or gold, but Christianizing peace.

Welcome the man of firm resolves, who never knew a fear,
Yet has a heart that nobly feels and does his best to cheer,

---

17 See note in "Most Respectfully Dedicated to the 73D, Late Louisiana Native
Guards"

The gallant sons of freemen upon the tented field,
May their reward be victory, and God their constant shield.

Welcome the warm, kind hearted friend of all the human race,
Whose hopes and aims have always been slavery to erase—
The only blot upon the shied of this enlightened land—
With men like him to clear the way it could no longer stand.

Welcome the man whose liberal views honor labor's right,
And with a hand of justice gives the black man and the white,
A code of laws, where they may work a great and glorious plan,
That draws them nearer to the truth, the noble rights of man.

Welcome the scholar and the man, whose nobleness of mind
Is felt throughout society so generous and refined;
And when the daily cares are done, around the social board,
He greets his friends with easy grace and frank and open word.

Welcome the man that dearly loves the sacred shrine of home—
The joy of every manly heart—'tis there he finds that boon,
Domestic bliss, confiding truth, each loving heart enshrine,
And children like the olive branch around the parent twine.

Welcome the lover of his country, who answered to the call,
That summoned out its legions to make foul treason fall;
God grant that it may soon be crushed into oblivion's night,
Then all our stars will glorious shine with freedom's sacred light.

Nathaniel Prentiss Banks was a celebrated Union general. During the Siege of Port Hudson (1863), he was the first to allow African Americans under his command to serve in battle. In the second stanza, the poet refers to Daniel Webster, a Massachusetts senator during the Civil War, Edward Everett, the chief speaker on the day Abraham Lincoln delivered the Gettysburg Address, and Charles Sumner, an abolitionist senator from Massachusetts.

In the Graveyard on the Hill

By Paul M. Russell
The Kansas Herald, February 6, 1880

I am sad at heart to-night
    And my spirit finds no rest,
For I miss the one who's gone
    To the region of the blest,
And when I am all alone,
    And the evening air is still,
Then I think of her who lies,
    In the graveyard on the hill.

When amid the festive throng,
    I performed my chosen part,
Though I sang the merry song,
    I was sad, indeed at heart;
For my truant thoughts would go,
    Where is peace and all is still
To that little grass-grown mound
    In the graveyard on the hill.

I was young when first the sod
    O'er that lovely form was laid;
I was young and I was gay
    Ere that lowly grave was made,
But my hopes of bliss are gone,
    And my mind doth wander still
To that little grass-grown mound
    In the graveyard on the hill.

Often when the evening shade,
          Hath o'spread the thirsty ground,
And the weary zephyrs made,
          Their last solitary sound;
While the cheering moonlights shone
          Over the vale and wood and rill;
I have mused beside that mound,
          In the graveyard on the hill.

But I know that there's an end
          To these many years of pain,
And I know that summer's sun
          Ne'er shall shine for me again,
But contented I will rest
          Where is peace and all is still;
By that little grass-grown mound
          In the graveyard on the hill.

To My Alice

*Two years have passed by since the tidings of Miss Alice Bowers'
death first startled her many friends. But no one felt the keen cut
made by the angel of death more than her devoted father, as the
following lines will attest.*

By T. J. B.
The Christian Recorder, November 20, 1884

How sad and lone I feel to-night,
     While thoughts of thee come o'er my heart;
Of thee so true, so pure and bright,
     Alas, how hard that we should part.

O, could I fold thee in my arms,
     And press my longing lips to thine,
With all thy bright and youthful charms,
     O, I would all the world resign.

I'll strew fresh flowers on thy tomb,
     My Alice dear, through love for thee;
I'll sing the songs in our sad home
     Thou oft did sing for love of me.

Ah! when for me this life shall end,
     O may we meet in heaven above,
Where bright immortal joys shall blend
     Our lives in never-ending love.

Marriage of an African American soldier; 1866

True Life

By R. J. Chiles
The Richmond Planet, February 21, 1885

Sitting in the quiet bliss,
Of true Love's first tender kiss,
They are sitting happy now;
They have pledged their mutual vow.

Both have in each others' eyes
Love's sweet meaning quickly caught;
And the time unheeded flies,
And the hour with joy is fraught.

For these two there is no turning,
In their lives and loves no break,
They will keep Hope's bright star burning,
Each Life's solemn duty take.

They have seen a loftier meaning,
In the love they pledged to-night,
Golden fruit from their lives gleaming,
They will Heaven keep in sight.

They'll remember at the altar,
All the sacred vows they made,
Both will keep them, neither falter,
In life's sunlight or its shade.

A Tribute to William C. Nell

Read by Miss Annie E. Smith at the Wm. C. Nell lecture
at the Zion A.M.E. Church, Boston, April 8, 1886.

By Elijah W. Smith
The New York Freeman, April 24, 1886

Behold! 'Mid picture of memory's wall,
Uncovered by dust or oblivion's pall,
Is his, true as steel, through the long, dreary night,
With his watch-fire burning, his sword ever bright,
It hangs by the side of the sweet, noble face
Of the great Liberator,[18] the pride of our race:
In that sanctified presence, a soft, holy spell
Illumines the features of William C. Nell.
With the love which King David to Jonathan[19] bore,
Our dear, sainted Garrison held him in store:
So ready for freedom to do and to dare,
The voice in the wilderness crying, "Prepare!"
O, true armor-bearer! the champion's call
Had rung through the land over cottage and hall;
And the hosts of the foe, with their banners of pride
Found thee faithful and fearless erect by his side.
With the eye of the seer in the future he saw
The certain fulfillment of heaven's great law;
That wrong, though victorious through the long night,
Must see, in the morning, the triumph of Right.
To millions unknown, yet he labored for all:

---

18 William Lloyd Garrison's influential antislavery newspaper, the *Liberator*.
19 See 1 & 2 Samuel, KJV.

His heart beat responsive to Liberty's call;
The poor, hunted fugitive found in his arms
A city[20] of refuge, secure from alarms.
It was his to remember and point to with pride,
The time and the cause for which brave Attucks[21] died;
To call on his people to honor the day
When the blood of the black man was shed in the fray.
For Liberty ne'er by submission was won;
The blast of the trumpet, the roar of the gun,
The shout of the 54th, clearing the way,
Rang the knell of oppression, proclaimed the glad day.
Oh! ne'er be it said, that, 'neath Freedom's bright sun,
We forgot the brave band who the struggle begun,
Who held up Hope's torch that the captive might see
Who battled and died that a race should be free.
Now the thunder of battle hath ceased on the plain,
And the old flag is waving unmarred by a stain,
Hail ye, who for us bore the ark of the free,
Fifty-fourth, Fifty-fifth, and Fifth Calvary.[22]
Long years have rolled by, and neglected, alone,
Lies the grave of a hero unmarked by a stone,
And the race in whose service his pure life was spent,
Pass by it unknown, unthinking, content.
But gratitude, long though her slumbers may be,
Shall awaken at last in the breast of the free,
And the children whose parents he labored to save,
Will bring their sad tributes to honor his grave.

---

20 Boston—Nell's birthplace and a city famously sympathetic to the antislavery
    cause.
21 Crispus Attucks, a fugitive slave and merchant seaman, was likely the first person
    slain in the 1770 Boston Massacre.
22 The 54th and 55th Regiments of the Massachusetts Volunteer Infantry were
    among the first African American combat units to serve in the Union Army and
    are noted for their extensive service and bravery. The men of the 5th United States
    Colored Cavalry are likewise remembered for their service and valor.

Peace, peace to his ashes! The trumpet of fame
Could not add to the glory encircling his name:
And, to us who have known him so long and so well,
How dear is the memory of William C. Nell.

*William Cooper Nell was an abolitionist, journalist, reformer, and author.
He worked for twenty-plus years with his friend and mentor William
Lloyd Garrison on the* Liberator, *was a co-founder of Frederick Douglass's*
North Star, *and authored* Services of Colored Americans in the Wars
of 1776 and 1812 *and* Colored Patriots of the American Revolution,
*two of the earliest extensive histories on African Americans' contributions as
servicemen. As a desegregationist, Nell was keenly interested in improving
both social and educational conditions for African American youth, and to
that end led the campaign that desegregated Boston's school system in 1855.
In 1857, in* Dred Scott v. Sandford, *the U.S. Supreme Court held that
African Americans were not citizens under the Constitution. As a nonviolent
response, Nell organized a memorial celebration of Revolutionary martyr
Crispus Attucks and established Crispus Attucks Day. He continued his
desegregation efforts during the Civil War, campaigning to have African
Americans accepted into the Union Army as combat soldiers. In 1861, Nell
became a postal clerk, becoming the first African American to serve in the
federal civil service. Nevertheless, he died relatively impoverished in 1874
and was buried in an unmarked grave. This poem was read at a memorial
celebration of Nell's life held to secure funds for a headstone, an effort that
for reasons unknown did not succeed. A monument was finally erected in
1989, 115 years after Nell's death.*

Bitter Sweet

By Rosa Hazel
The Savannah Weekly Echo, October 1, 1886

Oh my heart is sad to-night,
    With our parting grief and pain;
Flown has every vain delight—
    Lost seems every earthly gain.
Still we may reserve a joy,
    For in future we may meet;
Pleasure always has alloy—
    Bitter comes with every sweet.

Let us cheer the parting hour,
    Let us banish grief as vain;
Let us strive with all our power
    Soon to meet in joy again.
Though it may be far from here
    And in sorrow each may be,
Still to me you will be dear—
    Can you say the same to me?

If in days now passed away
    I have broken one sweet tie,
Think of me with charity—
    Never let it cause a sigh.
And while we linger here to-night,
    Each inspired with hope and love,
Let us here renew our plight,
    When we both may meet above.

Memorial Day

By Anonymous
The Benevolent Banner, May 28, 1887

With sound of solemn music,
    And men, in martial array,
Each bearing the flowers of springtime,
    Do we keep Memorial Day.
While hearts and drums are beating,
    And words of prayer are said,
Fair flowers, by faithful comrades' hands,
    On each soldier's grave are laid.

But the men who march to music,
    Each year are growing old;
And the number of graves is larger
    Each year in the churchyard cold,
And the time, that is surely coming,
    Will not many years delay,
When the last of our gray-haired veterans
    Will be tenderly laid away.

But when the last brave soldier
    Is buried beneath the sod,
The graves will still be covered
    With the fairest flowers of God.
For the spring will bring the daisy,
    And the autumn the golden rod,
And the wild rose will bloom in beauty
    Where once the soldiers trod.

While Memorial Day was not officially recognized as a federal holiday until 1971, memorial day celebrations first began following the close of the Civil War. By 1890 most states (both North and South) had adopted memorial day activities, usually held in May, to commemorate servicemen who died in the Civil War. As a current federal holiday, Memorial Day honors all military men and women who have given their lives in service.

A Short Journey

By The Ladies Dorcas Society
The Afro-American Advance, June 24, 1899

She is gone, but not forever,
      Mother's face will see again;
She has only crossed the river,
      And is resting free from pain.
Through the weary days of sickness,
      How she suffered none can tell.

But she's now within the city
      Where there never comes an ill.
Though our home is sad and lonely,
      And to us she ne'er can come,
In the future we shall greet her,
      When our journey here is done.

We miss thee from our home dear mother
      We miss thee from thy place;
A shadow o'er our life is cast—
      We miss the sunshine of thy face,
We miss thy kind and willing hand,
      Thy fond and earnest care—
Our home is dark without thee—
      We miss thee everywhere.

This poem is written in memory of Mrs. Lavinia Young of the Ladies Dorcas Society of the Bethesda Baptist Church, Minnesota.

III

Moral & Civic Perspectives

The Black Beauty

*Written from Solomon's Songs**

By Anonymous
Freedom's Journal, June 8, 1827

"Black, I am, oh! daughters fair,"
But my beauty is most rare;
Black, indeed, appears my skin,
Beauteous, comely, all within:
Black, when by affliction press'd,
Beauteous, when in Christ I rest;
Black, by sin's defiling flood.
Beauteous, wash'd in Jesus' blood:
Black, I am in mine own eyes,
Beauteous, in my Lord's I rise;
Black I am to men 'tis true;
Beauteous, in the angel's view:
Black, if Jesus frowns awhile,
Beauteous, when I see him smile;
Black, while in the tomb I lie,
Beauteous, when I mount the sky!

*See Song of Solomon 1:5 (KJV)

Sonnet to Adversity

By Anonymous
The Colored American, April 17, 1841

Thou art a harsh instructor—yet by thee
    We learn important lessons; thou dost teach
How frail and fleeting earthly hopes may be
    How oft the goal recedes we strive to reach;
Thine is a form of darkness, and we turn
    Heart-sick and weary from the sad embrace,
Would fly thy dreaded presence, ever stern,
    And, trembling, hide us from thy frowning face.
But thro' the world's dim pathway thy cold hand
    Is leading to a home of joy and peace,
And on the borders of that better land
    Will thy sharp ministry forever cease;
And we shall bless thee safely landed there,
And know in heaven how good thy teachings were.

The Temperance Banner

By Anonymous
Freedom's Advocate, April 7, 1842

Now the Temperance banner is waving
  In the open air, and free;
Many thousands now are gathering,
  Not to arms, but victory!

Victory over that dread monster
  Which hath his ten commandments slain,
More than all the blood and carnage
  Of a Napoleon's reign!

Alcohol, whate'er its color,
  Is the Tyrant in disguise;
Then no more the bane we'll coret,
  But from vice to virtue rise.

The hydra-head we soon shall conquer;
  Our breastplate be the judge;
If a victory is ne'er recorded,
  Ne'er on ancient history's page.

Rescue! rescue! is the watchword
  Of the gallant temperance band;
Rally around us, we will save you
  From the ruthless tyrant's hand!

Cry of freedom! wave your banners,
     Wave them high in open air,
Where every eye may see portrayed
     The Father of his country there.

Look on This Picture, and Then on That

By M. R.
The Northern Star and Freeman's Advocate, April 7, 1842

A mother sat beside the hearth,
    The burning brands were few;
And through the broken window-pane
    The bitter night-wind blew:
Upon her breast a cherub babe
    Had sobbed itself to sleep,
And standing at her side, a boy
    With heart too proud to weep.

He twined his little arms around
    A sister's fragile form,
And whispered words of manly cheer,
    As louder blew the storm.
"Weep not," he cried, "the storm will cease,
    Rest here thy aching head;
Oh, do not weep! Papa will come,
    He'll come and give us bread."

Why flow the tears, like summer rain,
    Adown that mother's cheek?
Why throbs her heart with agony
    Her lips may not bespeak?
Weeps she the stately halls of youth,
    Changed for the lowly cot?
Or want, or woe, or winter's cold,
    Or loneliness of lot?

It is not cold, nor pinching want,
  That dims that azure eye;
Nor is it care or weariness
  That prompts the bitter sigh.
'Tis, that the father of her babes
  Is but a sire in name—
She weeps her children's heritage
  Of infamy and shame.

She weeps the thought-dispelling draught,
  That, with a syren's charms,
Hath lured the father from his home—
  The husband from her arms.
She weeps the bitter tears that fall,
  Upon a living tomb;
And earth hath nothing more to give
  Of misery or gloom.

   * * * * * * *

The scene is changed,—a mother sits
  Beside the blazing hearth;
And oft the cheerful cottage rings
  To sounds of infant mirth.
The white-washed wall, the sanded floor,
  The table neatly spread,
The casement lined with verdant shrubs,
  The snow-white pallet bed.

The bolted shutter, that defies
  The winter's cold so well,
And the happy light of joyous eyes,
  Content and comfort tell.
Calm beauty on that mother's brow

Rests, like the bow of peace
That only decks the summer skies
        When fearful tempests cease.

Whose form is that, to which her eye
        Oft turns in conscious joy?
It is the parent of her babes—
        The father of her boy!
He has dashed aside the tempting cup
        That lured him forth to roam;
And peace and plenty smile again
        Upon his cottage home.

Loving and loved, his prattling ones
        By turns now share his knee,
And tell by turns the happy tale
        Of artless infancy.
The very house-dog on the hearth
        Looks up with smiling face;
With piteous moan he seeks to share
        His playmates' warm embrace.

Oh wedded love! when at the hearth
        Thy circle fondly meet,
And heart gives back to answering heart
        The warm responsive beat,
Earth hath no scene like thine below,
        To mirror that above:
Thou art the only emblem, here
        Of Heaven's unfading love.

A Child's Appeal

By Cynthia Hall
The Northern Star and Freeman's Advocate, December 8, 1842

This pledge, dear father, won't you sign,
    And once more happy be?
The drunkard's cup won't you resign,
    And come, rejoice with me?
O father, 'tis a fearful sight
    To see your crimson face,
And the wild billow, black as night,
    Bear you to deep disgrace.

Father! harsh words you sometimes speak,
    How dismal to my ear!
Your eyes strike dread when mine they meet,
    And cause me much to fear.
O father! once it was not so;
    Once love beamed in your eye;
Your voice, how charming, none can tell,
    Or tender your reply.

But now 'tis changed! No accents sweet
    Fall from your lips to me;
Your child, with threatening tones you greet;
    O father! must this be?
You know there is a heaven above,
    Where drunkards cannot go;
A heaven of happiness and love,
    Without one pang of woe.

Father! I'm going to that land,
      Say, will you stay behind?
You cannot join the heavenly band
      Till you've the *cup* resigned.
Say, must I bid for a long farewell
      To a father dear as mine?
My agony—O none can tell!
      Say, father! WON'T YOU SIGN?

Mother! the pledge I know *you'll* sign,
      I feel that it must be;
My proffered hand, *you'll* not decline,
      But strive for heaven with me.
Then in that bright and blissful land,
      We'll every care resign,
And join the sweet harmonious band—
      O, father, mother, SIGN!

The Daughter's Prayer

By T. A. Shea
The Northern Star and Freeman's Advocate, December 8, 1842

Why so pale that maiden's cheek;
    Why that bosom lifted high,
As beneath the heart would break
    With the anguish of its sigh?

She, alas! has lived to see,
    Sight of woe—her father's shame,
And his brow—oh misery!
    Branded with a drunkard's name.

At morn and evening, day by day,
    In her chamber, at the shrine,
Does she for that father pray
    With a fervency divine.

Oh! She loves him truthfully,
    He had been her morning star,
Ever guiding tempest-free
    O'er life's treacherous seas afar.

But with slow and stealthy pace
    Came the spirit-demon up,
And with smile of social grace
    Bade him drain the festive cup.

That frail moment was the last
  To her heart of cloudless light,
How could darkness come so fast
  O'er a scene so fair and bright?

Swift destruction followed there;
  Not a relic, not a trace
Of his virtues once so rare,
  Linger'd in their dwelling place.

But that daughter's prayer arose
  In acceptance to the throne;
And the mountain weight of woes
  By her faith was overthrown.

Loving thus the Roman's Daughter
  Buoy'd him with her bosom's wave;
Sooth'd him with the breath he brought her,
  Fed him with the life he gave.

Spurn not then the mortal straying
  From the safety of the fold;
But the gentle force of praying
  In this father sav'd behold!

Speak Not a Bitter Word

By M. C. [Columbus, Ohio]
The Palladium of Liberty, June 26, 1844

Wouldst thou a wanderer reclaim,
A wild and artless spirit tame?
Check the warm flow of youthful blood,
And lead a lost one back to God?
Pause, if thy spirit's wrath be stirred,
Speak not to him a bitter word.
Speak not! that bitter word may be
The stamp that seals his destiny.

If wildly he hath gone astray,
And dark excess has marked his way;
'T is pitiful—but yet beware!
Reform must come from kindly care;
Forbid thy parting lips to move,
But in the gentle tones of love;
Though sadly his young heart hath erred,
Speak not to him a bitter word.

The lowering frown he will not bear,
The venom'd chidings, will hear;
The ardent spirit will not brook
The stinging touch of sharp rebuke.
Thou wouldst not goad the restless steed,
To calm his fire or check his speed;
Then let no angry tones be heard,
Speak not to him a bitter word.

Go kindly to him—make him feel,
Your heart yearns deeply for his weal;
Tell him the dangers thick that lay,
Around his wildly devious way. —
So shalt thou win him, call him back,
From pleasures smoothe seductive track;
And warnings thou hast mildly given,
May guide the wanderer up to Heaven.

Family services in South Carolina

Fearless and Faithful

By J. C. O. [Onondaga County, New York]
The North Star, January 5, 1849

Labor fearless, labor faithful,
    Labor while the day shall last,
For the shadows of the evening
    Soon the sky will overcast;
Ere shall end thy day of labor,
    Ere shall rest thy manhood's sun,
Strive with every power within thee,
    That the appointed task be done.

Life is not a trackless shadow,
    Nor the wave upon the beach;
Though our days are brief, yet lasting
    Is the stamp we give to each.
"Life is real, life is earnest,"
    Full of labor, full of thought;
Every hour and every moment
    Is with living vigor fraught.

Fearless wage life's sternest conflict,
    Faithful to thy high trust,
If thou'lt have a memory cherished,
    And a path bright as the just.
Labor fearless, labor faithful,
    Labor until the set of sun,
And welcome shall await thee,
    Promised plaudit of "Well done!"

A Song

By William Wallace
The North Star, March 16, 1849

Where is my Native Land?
　　Where the East sparkles?
Where the wide, wooded West
　　By the sea darkles?
Where the soft, sunny South,
　　Like a bride glowing,
Sees the proud sun in state
　　To her couch going?
　　　Where is my Native Land?

　　That is my Native Land
Where the East sparkles;
　　Where the wide, wooded West
By the sea darkles.
　　South and the North! alike
Ye claim my being;
　　All races are the same
To the All-seeing.
　　Down with the feudal lie!
Man is my brother;
　　God is my Father, and
Earth is my Mother.
　　The World is my native land!

Martial Glory

By Anonymous
The North Star, August 17, 1849

Oh! meteor, whose delusive beams
　　　But glitter brightly to betray,
Misleading with thy dazzling gleams
　　　The steps of many far astray;
Oh! guiding star of many a heart,
I view thee as thou truly art—
A *wisp*, which glimmers through the gloom
That rests upon the gaping tomb.

The gaudy flag which proudly streams
Within the morning's golden beams,
Or flutters through the crimson mist
　　　Which veils the battle on its flight,
Seeming to those who still exist,
　　　The beacon of the bloody fight—
The splendid uniforms which make
　　　But brighter marks for blade and ball—
The strains of melody which wake
　　　A courage in the hearts of all,
And leads the soldier, faint with pain,
O'er bodies of his comrades slain,
All heedless of the whizzing shot
That falls around him fast and hot—
The medals and the flaming stars
Thou hangest on the veteran's scars,
Those toys for which the grown-up child

Risks life and limb, by thee beguiled.

Thou dost enwreath by votaries' brows,
   With laurels which I envy not,
For they were gathered from those boughs
   Which grew upon some mournful spot,
Whose soil was ploughed by cannon balls,
And watered by the stream which falls
From bleeding wounds, while through the cloud
Of sulphurous smoke which thundered loud,
The bullets, with resistless power,
Were hailing their destructive shower.

Oh! I would live and die alone,
   If such should be the will of God,
And unlamented and unknown,
   Repose beneath the tombless sod,
And leave no memory on the earth
To tell the future I had birth,
Like some lost billow, of whose sweep
No vestige lingers on the deep,
Rather than wear around my name,
That infamy which men call fame—
That red renown which stains the page
   Of history with the lives of those
Who, demon-like, in every age,
Have filled the earth with warfare's woes.

Sonnet

By A. S. Standard
Frederick Douglass' Paper, July 31, 1851

You should not speak to think, nor think to speak;
But words and thoughts should of themselves outwell
From inner fullness; Chest and heart should swell
To give them birth. Better be dumb a week
Than idly prattle; better in leisure sleek
Lie fallow-minded, than a brain compel
To wasting plenty that hath yielded well,
Or strive to crop a soil too thin and bleak.
One thought from the deep heart upspringing,
May from within a whole life fertilize;
One true word, like the lightning sudden gleaming,
May rend the night a whole world of lies.
Much speech, much thought, may often be but seeming,
But in one Truth might boundless ever lies.

The True Hero

By A. R. [Jamestown, New York]
Frederick Douglass' Paper, February 5, 1852

It is his aim,
To travel on in duty's way,
　　Though multitudes defame—
His motives constantly gainsay.

He labors on,
Undaunted by the world's dark frown:
　　Prepared to suffer wrong,
It cannot weigh his spirit down.

Ever awake
The pangs of sorrow to allay,
　　No enemy can shake,
Or lead him from his course astray.

He firmly stands
Where poisoned arrows round him fly;
　　Where virtue aid demands,
He fights to conquer or to die.

Unmoved by fear,
Though envy may diffuse her bane,
　　Or malice toil severe,
To heap reproach upon his name.

He finds within,
A true and never-failing guide:
    There is on earth for him
No monitor so safe beside.

    And when life wanes,
Its tender cords are nearly riven,
    He finds what well sustains,
And aids him in his flight to Heaven.

Christ and Mars—Or Christianity and War

By D. M. KELSEY [Geneva, Illinois]
Frederick Douglass' Paper, March 25, 1852

"Trust the Lord, and keep your powder dry,"
Said Cromwell,[23] when along the darkened sky,
Flew forth the swift-winged messenger of fate,
Which sent a multitude to Pluto's gate!
Trust in the Lord, and pray, "Our Father, God,"
Then smite his children with a demon's rod!
Breathe forth thy prayer, "Most hallowed be Thy name,
Thy Kingdom come, Thy will be done, the same
On earth, as heaven;" then ope the cannon's mouth.
Let slip the dogs of hell, from North to South!
From East to West, let fiends incarnate rage!
And make mankind, in warlike scenes engage,
Trust in the Lord, to "give you daily bread,"
And eat your food with hands by murder red!
"Forgive us, Lord, as we our foes forgive,"
Then rob them of those joys for which they live!
"Into temptation, lead us not, Oh! Lord,"
But give us hearts to kill with grape[24] and sword!
"From every form of evil, set us free,"
But help us fill the earth with crimsoned sea!
"And unto Thee, shall glory, honor, power,
And praise be given," when in a direful hour,
The lights of Heaven shall fade, amid the glare

---

23   Oliver Cromwell was 1st Lord Protector of the Commonwealth of England,
     Scotland and Ireland, 1653–1658.
24   Grapeshot

Of universal fires; and demons wear
The crown of undistinguished right and sway!
Such is the scene where CROMWELLS rule the day;
And such the past, that CHRISTIAN WARRIORS play!

Oliver Cromwell was instrumental in England's Civil War and was a signer of King Charles I's death warrant. A fervently religious Protestant, Cromwell's campaigns against Catholics (especially in Ireland and Scotland) were untellably brutal. In this poem, Kelsey reflects on killing in the name of God; the prayer quoted throughout is the Lord's Prayer.

Work While It Is Called To-Day

By J. A. Langford [Philadelphia, Pennsylvania]
Frederick Douglass' Paper, September 10, 1852

Work while the day is,
      Wait for no morrow,
Life else a prey is,
      To dreaming and sorrow.

Doing and duty
      Will gladden the hour,
Giving earth beauty
      And joy for her dower.

Twelve hours are given
      Then faithfully use
The bounty which heaven
      To none doth refuse.

The storms of life breasting,
      As swimmers the sea,
"Unhasting, unresting,"
      Thy motto should be.

No talent concealing
      In darkness or dust;
God giveth no feeling
      For mildew and rust.

No effort withholding,
     A brother to bless;
'Tis heaven unfolding,
     Thus onward to press.

Free leisure is doing
     The duties of life;
Working is wooing
     Sweet peace from the strife.

Then work while the day is,
     Wait for no morrow,
Life else a prey is,
     To dreaming and sorrow.

A day's honest labor; circa 1862

Colonization

By Martin Cross [Catskill, New York]
Frederick Douglass' Paper, April 8, 1853

Talk not to me of Colonization,
For I'm a *freeman* of this nation.
Then why forsake my native land
For Afric's burning sun and sand?
We hereby make our proclamation,
That we're opposed to emigration
This is the land which gave us birth—
Our father's graves are freedom's earth;
They won the freedom they enjoy,
How can you freemen's rights destroy?
We, to a man, determined stand
To ne'er forsake our native land.
Then away, say we, to Colonization,
But give us God—emancipation;
Success attend our holy cause—
Our motto—"God and righteous laws."
Then, friends of Colonization, give o'er
Nor strive to drive us from this shore;
For we're determined to a man
Not to forsake our native land—
Where bright Emancipation gleams—
Where Freedom's banner o'er us streams;
We've borne its stripes of crimson hue,
We'll share its stars' proud glory too!

The Colonization movement, which encouraged free people African descent to return to Africa (or, in some instances, to emigrate to Haiti), began in the earlier part of the century. In the 1830s in particular, thousands of free African Americans relocated to an uncolonized region on the western coast of Africa; with the aid of the American Colonization Society, these emigrants established the country of Liberia in 1847. However, many African Americans, most of whom were generations removed from Africa, felt that America was their homeland and opposed the colonization movement.

"A Political Discussion"; 1868

Friendship

By J. C. HOLLY Rochester, New York
Frederick Douglass' Paper, November 24, 1854

Ah! endearing word! celestial emanation!
Oft uttered by false lips, the portals of foul hearts,
Who, with their tongues profane, blaspheme thy sacred name,
Making the heart grow sick, and hope to sink within.
But yet, thou art not all an airy phantom, who,
Like some will-o'-wisp leads on the weary foot
Through gloomy swamps, to the dark regions of despair;
Thou hast a touch stone true, which, like Ithuriel's spear,
Proves which is pure or base.
Yes poverty! stern poverty! thou art that spear;
And when like swift-winged swallows, on an autumn day,
Friends coolly take their leave, thy point hath done its work,
Transformed the swelling toads.

True Friendship! angelic being! glides into the hut
And warms its shiv'ring inmates with her genial breath:
Unlike the baser kind, when the leaves of autumn
Leave bare the arms of oak and elm, and spread the ground;
Through frost and snow alike, her gentle feet are heard
Amidst the many false, who, like to summer flies,
Have thronged my path, I've met with friendship true,
Throwing her warm mantle o'er my shiv'ring neck,
And filling my scanty store with ample portion;
Making the heart glad, and the hearth to smile with cheer,
The bleached snow to look less cold, and the stars more bright,
The storm less hard to bear,

Such friendship is of origin divine—earth's salt—
Cooling the parched fever, warning the dull ague,
Patching the worn garment, and serving every need
That human nature sore, afflicted suf'ring feels.

Our Voices

By T. A. Shea
The Weekly Anglo-African, March 1859

Once again to thee, Temperance an anthem we'll raise,
And tell of thy triumph in song;
Once again will our voices unite in thy praise,
And echo thy triumph prolong.

We will tell of the blessings, thy light has bestowed
On the homes that were lonely and sad,
Of the smiles that now beam where the tear often flowed,
Where the hearts that were mourning, are glad.

Like an angel of light, thou hast sped through the earth,
Bidding Hope take the place of Despair;
Thou hast changed the rude oath and the reveler's mirth,
To the voice of thanksgiving and prayer.

The poor wretched outcast, once treated with scorn,
Thou hast sought to restore and reclaim,
And hundreds thus rescued, shall live to adorn,
And brighten thy record of Fame.

Battle With Life

By Lansford Lane
The Weekly Anglo-African, March 1859

Bear thee up bravely,
  Strong heart and true,
Meet thy woes gravely,
  Strive with them too!
Let them not win from thee
  Tears of regret;
Such were a sin for thee—
  Hope for good yet!

Rouse thee from drooping,
  Care-laden soul,
Mournfully stooping
  'Neath grief's control!
Far o'er the gloom that lies
  Shrouding the earth,
Light from eternal skies
  Shows us thy worth.

Nerve thee yet stronger,
  Resolute mind;
Let care no longer
  Heavily bind.
Rise only thy eagle-wings,
  Gloriously free,
Till from material things,
  Pure thou shalt be!

Bear ye up bravely,
    Soul and mind too!
Droop not so gravely,
    Bold heart and true!
Clear rays of streaming light
    Shine through the gloom;
God's love is beaming bright,
    E'en round the tomb.

Gordon, a penniless fugitive slave, upon enlisting
in the Union Army to fight for freedom; 1863

He's None the Worse for That

By Mrs. E. Coutee
The Weekly Anglo-African, July 30, 1859

What though the homespun suit he wears—
    Best suit to the sons of toil—
What though no coarser food he fares,
    And tends the loom, or tills the soil;
What though no gold-leaf gilds the tongue,
    Devoted to congenial chat—
If right prevails, and not the wrong,
    The man is none the worse for that.

What though within the humble cot,
    No costly ornament is seen;
What though the wife possesses not
    Her satin gowns of black and green;
What though the merry household band
    Half-naked fly to ball and bat;
If conscience guide the head and heart,
    The man is none the worst for that.

Truth is not a thing of dress—
    Of splendor, wealth, or classic lore;
Would that these wrappings were loved less,
    And honest worth was clung to more!
Though pride may spurn the toiling crowd,
    The tattered garb, the crownless hat,
Yet God and nature cry aloud,
    The man is none the worse for that.

Live Bravely

By James Rochelle
The Weekly Anglo-African, December 10, 1859

The world is half-darkened with croakers,
      Whose burdens are weighing them down;
They croak of their stars and ill-usage,
      And grope in the ditch for a crown.
Why talk to the wind of thy fortune,
      Or clutch at distinction and gold?
If thou canst not reach high on the ladder,
      Thou canst steady its base by thy hold.

For the flower, thon hidist in the corner
      Will as faultlessly finish its bloom,
Will reach for a sparkle of sunshine,
      That clouds have not chanced to consume;
And wouldst thou be less than a flower,
      With thought, and a brain, and a hand?
Wilt wait for the dripples of fortune,
      When there is something that these may command?

There is a food to be won from the furrow,
      And forests that wait to be hewn;
There is marble untouched by the chisel,
      Days that break not on the forehead of June.
Will you let the plow rust in the furrow—
      Unbuilded, a house or a hall—
Nor bid the stones wake from their silence,
      And fret as if fretting were all?

Go learn from the blossoms and ant-hills,
      There's something thy labor must give;
Like the beacon that pierces the tempest,
      Strike the clod from thy footing, and live.
Live—not trail with thy face in the dross-heap,
      In the track of the brainless and proud:
Lift the cerements away from thy manhood—
      Thou art robbing the dead of a shroud.

There are words and pens to be wielded,
      There are thoughts that must die if unsaid;
Wouldst thou saunter and pine amid roses,
      Or sepulchre dreams that are dead?
No! drag the hope to the pyre—
      Dreams dead from the ashes will rise;
Look not down on earth for its shadow,
      There is sunlight for thee in the skies.

Be Content

By Cynthia Bayou

The Weekly Anglo-African, January 1860

Mistaken mortal, ever fretting,
Grasping, grinding, groaning, getting,
    Be content!

If thou hast enough, be thankful,
Just as if thou had a bankful,
    Be content!

If fortune cast thy lot but humble,
Earn thy bread and do not grumble,
    Be content!

Have the rich, thinkst thou, no trouble?
Twice thy wealth, thy sorrows double,
    Be content!

List the lyre of learned sages—
Those wise men of the Grecian ages,
    Be content!

Their reckoning up of all earth's riches,
Was compressed in one short phrase, which is,
    Be content!

The rich man gets, with all his heaping,
But dress, and drink, and food, and sleeping,
    Be content!

Though in sleep the rich men gain not,
Poor men sleep when rich men may not,
    Be content!

Remember, thou for wealth who rakest,
"Nought thou broughtest, nought thou takest,"
    Be content!

Never Give Up

By Anonymous
The Concordia Eagle, April 1, 1882

Never give up while yet there's life,
Never give way to toil and strife,
Never give up; skies may be dark;
Wait, and rise with the early lark,
For after night of dark despair,
Brightness of morning will be there.

Never give up, it will not pay;
Keep your eyes open, watch and pray;
Rush onward, hope, and look ahead,
Never give up till daylight's sped,
For darkest clouds have a silver lining,
Across the deep the stars are shining.

Never give up; life is but work;
The goal is not reached by those who shirk,
Whatever you do, do with a will,
And you'll surmount the difficult hill
And rise upon the wings of fame
Till the world shall echo to you a name.

Then despair not, for clouds may fly,
Even between the brightest sky,
But look forward—there glory waits—
Just beyond are the eternal gates,
But while climbing the hill you cannot know
What pleasures are in the valley below.

Compensation

By Florence Bronson Tucker
The Negro World, October 20, 1884

Through clouds that skim the darkening sky
    We best can see the sun,
Up rugged steeps in life's hard ways,
    Are noblest victories won.

The iron plowshare's shining blade
    More fertile makes the field;
The grain that's hardest threshed, in truth,
    Most precious harvests yield.

Down mountain heights, o'er stony beds,
    The purest waters flow;
Each saintly life, each conquering hand,
    The cross of pain must know.

To spirits grieved and hearts that ache
    The sweetest songs are born;
The nightingale in darkened cage
    Sings first to greet the morn.

From the fair bloom the foot has crushed
    Flagrant perfumes arise;
Fair are the visions Heaven grants
    To dim and sightless eyes.

Be still, O Soul! into God's hand
          Thy richest treasures give;
Subject to His unerring will
          Shalt thou most nobly live.

Emigrate

By H. Lavell
Western Cyclone, July 1886

John and Ben were sturdy sons of toil,
    Who filled poor old Indiana's soil;
'Tis said they traced their pedigree
    Back to the well known brothers three,
Who, in September, crossed the Mississippi,
    From debt, to be free.

So they resolved to try their fate,
    And to the west would emigrate;
They fixed on Kansas as the spot
    Where they would cast their future lot,
And when to the their western home they got,
    It suit their fancy, to a dot.

John and Ben spent many years of toil,
    In cultivating eastern soil
But now, light-hearted joyous tones
    Replace their old time weary groans,
When they compare the land they own
    With that so full of stumps and stones.

To all who want a Kansas home,
    We extend a cordial welcome,
Seven dollars an acre will buy
    The finest land beneath the skies.
Come and see us, we'll tell you why,
    This means business by and bye.

Sympathy

By Lewis Howard Latimer [New York, New York]
The New York Age, September 20, 1890

Within the heart of each and all,
A hidden recess lies;
Wherein some secret sorrow rests,
The source of all their sighs.
A blighted hope; ambition's wreck;
A love-like withered flower,—
Bearing in death a fragrance still,
That giveth it a power,
To sweeten yet with its faint breath
Of love's bright summer day,
The moments given to regret
For joys now passed away.
Some bear their load with troubled brow;
Some wear a smiling face,
As tho' no care within their hearts
Could find a resting place:
But each and every thirsty soul
Will filled with comfort be;
And bless the hand that gives to them
A kindly sympathy.

Which

By S. H. Johnson
Historic Times, September 26, 1891

A problem faces you and I,
And we can solve it if we try.
But many ways must go for naught
If we could solve it as we ought.

Will wide-mouthed bluster on the street
The great demand for answer meet?
Will stygian gloom of intellect
Help us to do the "sum" correct?

Will ceaseless flaunt of past disgrace
Exalt us with the stronger race?
Will halls of learning always be
A "factor" which we fail to see?

Will banks always to us be strange,
And commerce deemed beyond our range?
Will unknown land or star or sea
Be brought to light by you or me?

Will we receive like so much alms
Just what is placed into our palms?
Nor seek nor search like other men
Who "beard the lion in his den"?

Or, will we take a wiser plan
And our surroundings closely scan?
And study cause and then effect
Then pause to ponder and reflect?

And come to see as others can,
That brains and dollars make the man?
Of these two ways, the timely "stitch,"
Pray tell me reader, is found in "which"?

In the years following the Civil War there was a movement, largely spearhead-ed by benevolent societies, towards educating freed peoples. With emancipation came the fundamental right of freedom, but many freed people—formerly entirely dependent on their owners and completely uneducated—lacked the basic skills to navigate society successfully. In this poem, Johnson is reflecting on the need for continued and greater education among African Americans.

SEA-ISLAND SCHOOL, No. 1.—ST. HELENA ISLAND. ESTABLISHED APRIL, 1862.

TEACHERS { MISS LAURA M. TOWNE,
" ELLEN MURRAY.
MRS. HARRIOT W. RUGGLES.

Supported by the Pennsylvania Branch.

EDUCATION AMONG THE FREEDMEN.

Set Yer Teeth an' Come Agin!

By Anonymous
The Afro-American Advance, September 16, 1899

Don't loaf around an' kick when luck
Don't seem to come your way, but buck
Agin adversity till you
Through breakin' clouds kin see the blue.
Don't think because the skies are black
The sun has jumped his job, but stack
Yer nerve all in a bunch to win
An' set yer teeth an' come agin!

In every life some rain must fall,
In every sweet there is some gall,
An' every earthly trail of ours
Must have some thorns among the flowers.
If fortune treats you rather rough
Look on its coldness as a bluff;
At every knockdown wear a grin
An' set yer teeth an' come agin!

The man who wins success mus' fight
His way up fortune's rocky height,
Mus' battle bravely day by day,
An' never loiter by the way.
Reverses of'n come; the foe
Will deal you many a stunnin' blow,
But solid nerve is bound to win—
Jes' set yer teeth an' come agin!

The field o' life is thickly strewn
With men who lost their nerve too soon,
Who lacked the gritty nerve to stay
An' give an' take in many way.
Choose fur yer motto: "Win or die!"
When sent to grass don't never lie
An' sadly say; "It might have bin!"
But set yer teeth an' come agin!

When you have reached the goal at last,
With not a cloud to overcast
Yer sky of life, when, day by day,
All things jes' seem to fall your way,
Then you kin take yer lazy ease,
Kin loaf around jes' as you please,
An' then you'll say with cheery grin;
"I set my teeth an' come agin!"

IV

Reminiscence & Humor

There Was a Time I Never Sighed

"Did not I weep for him that was in trouble?
Was not my soul grieved for the poor?" (Job 30:25; KJV)

By C. E. E.
Freedom's Journal, April 6, 1827

There was a day I never sigh'd;
    There was a time I gladly sung:
Oh, how I wish I had died,
    When mind was pure and form was young.

If I were well, a father stoop'd,
    Above my bed, to bless my sleep;
If I were ill, a mother droop'd,
    And left my couch to think and weep.

My playmates were as brothers tried;
    Yes, winter days had sunshine then;
I could not tell why people sigh'd;
    Nor feel the cares of busy men.

Friends I have had, as kind and brave
    As ever shared a pliant soul:
But now, affection's foe, the grave,
    Has made the floods of sorrow roll.

And I have lost my tide, my time;
    Cast off the robe of innocence;
Have nurtur'd pride; encourag'd crime;
    Ah! flung away my best defence.

Repentance hangs upon my heart;
　　Sweet thoughts for all are in my mind;
I would not throw a venom'd dart—
　　O! no, I never was unkind!

Yet, when my stream of tears is wide,
　　My willow'd harp to this is strung:
"O, how I wish I had died,
　　When mind was pure and form was young."

Moveing Day

By Anonymous
Freedom's Journal, May 4, 1827

I've seen an army put to rout,
And whole battalions turn about,
  And flee away from trouble;
And I have seen great towns ransack'd,
And lofty spires by earthquakes rack'd,
  And thought them a mere bubble.

But Oh! I've seen with trembling fear,
The dreadful moveing day draw near,
  With all its sad vexation;
When dire confusion rules the day,
And female power usurps the sway,
  As if it were a nation.

When broken fragments strow the way,
And tables, chairs, in dread array,
  Are pil'd upon each other;
And kettles, pots, in one great heap,
Thrown in with beds and glasses, keep
  Up one perpetual bother.

The "Washing-Day" is far more fair,
I witness it without "despair,"
  For there is no reproving;
But Oh! I hope I ne'er again,
Shall be compell'd to feel the pain,
  The agony of moveing.

On the Poetic Muse

By George M. Horton [Chatham County, North Carolina]
Freedom's Journal, August 29, 1828

Far, far above the world I soar,
And almost nature lose,
Aerial regions to explore
With this ambitious muse.

My tow'ring thoughts with pinions rise
Upon the gales of song,
Which waft me through the mental sky
With music on my tongue.

My muse is all on mystic fire
Which kindles in my breast,
To scenes remote, she doth aspire
As never get expressed.

Wrapt in the dust, she scorns to lie
Call'd by new charms away,
Nor will she ever refuse to try
Such wonders to survey.

Such is the quiet bliss of soul
When in some lone retreat,
Where pensive thoughts like streamlets roll
And render silent sweet.

And when the vain tumultuous crowd
Shakes comfort from my mind,
My muse ascends above the cloud
And leaves the noise behind.

With vivid flight she mounts on high
Above the dusky maze,
And with perspicacious eye
Doth far from nature gaze.

Misconstrued

By Lunsford Lane
Freedom's Press, February 1842

He was a city fellow;
      She was a girl from Maine;
She had black eyes, was pretty,
      While he was rath'r plain.
She spoke of her old homestead
      Down in her native town;
"I love your country manors,"
      He murmured, with a frown.

She felt somewhat insulted
      At what the fellow said:
She'd studied for a twelvemonth
      To appear city bred.
She tossed her head in anger
      And shook her raven curls;
"Please keep *your city manna*
      To give to other girls."

They parted with resentment,
      With meanings misconstrued;
She thought him very saucy;
      He thought her rath'r rude.
She thought that *he* meant *manner*;
      He thought *she* meant the same;
And for this painful parting
      Our language is to blame.

Storms on Life's Ocean

By T. A. Gould
The North Star, December 8, 1848

The child 'neath rosy skies of morning,
    Trims his vessel's tiny sail;
His joyous laugh, all peril scorning,
    Mingles with the wooing gale.

He dreameth not of care or sadness;
    The world to him is fair and bright—
High his bosom swells with gladness;
    Flowers of pleasure bless his sight.

Years have passed. And stern emotion
    Sits upon that changing brow:
"There are storms on life's dark ocean,"
    He must learn that lesson now.

Years have passed. That bark is driving
    Bravely on its swift career;
The youth to manhood grown is striving
    With new dangers ever near.

Firm his hand the helm is guiding;
    He is watchful; but his breast,
Once so trustful and confiding,
    Now with care is deep opprest.

Years have passed. And stern emotion
      Broods upon his world-worn brow;
"There are storms on life's dark ocean,"
      He hath learned that lesson now.

Years have passed. Behold that battered
      Lonely vessel floating past;
The sails are torn, the spars are shattered
      By the lightning and the blast.

In the broken bark reposing,
      Mark that old and feeble form;
His busy scenes at last are closing,
      Scenes of sunshine and of storm.

His eyes are raised in calm devotion—
      Faith now smoothes his aged brow;
"There are storms on life's dark ocean,"
      Well he knows the lesson now.

Delusive Hope

By James Monroe Whitfield [Buffalo, New York]
Frederick Douglass' Paper, November 12, 1852

In the bright days of early youth
    Hope told a fond, delusive tale,
Of lasting friendship, holy truth,
    And steadfast love which ne'er should fail.

I listened to the flattering strain
    With all the fire of ardent youth;
And long I sought, but sought in vain,
    To find the dwelling place of Truth.

Though many in her garb appeared,
    Assumed her name and simple mien,
Ere long the vile deceit was cleared,
    And all the hypocrite was seen.

And Friendship, too, though long and loud,
    Her voice I've heard in many a place,
Among the fickle, thoughtless crowd,
    I never have beheld her face.

Love next its bright and glittering chain
    Around the captive fancy threw;
But soon its vows proved false and vain
    As the chameleon's changeful hue.

Now, when the hopes and joys are dead
        That gladdened once the heart of youth,
All the romantic visions fled
        That told of Friendship, Love and Truth.

Turn we unto that steadfast friend
        Who guards our steps where'er they move,
Whose power supports us to the end,
        Whose word is truth, whose name is love.

Grief

By J. C. Holly [Rochester, New York]
Frederick Douglass' Paper, September 29, 1854

Oh! tell me! who hath tasted not,
  The agonizing cup of grief?
Whose heart hath not a tender spot,
  Which urge the tears to its relief?

Oh! tell me! who hath never felt
  Emotions kindred to despair—
Whose grief in tears refuse to melt,
  Rush to the heart and canker there?

Yet, when beneath the blow we're bowed,
  And all around seems gloom and night,
Serene behind the darkest cloud,
  The star of Hope shines ever bright.

It shines alas! but still 'tis true,
  To grope in darkness is our doom;
The cloud obscures it from our view—
  Our filling eyes can't pierce the gloom.

Then let us ever put our trust
  In One who can our grief assuage;
At whose mandate the tempest must
  Curb in its breath, and cease to rage.

The Past

Il passato e passato, e per sempre![25]

By Anonymous
Frederick Douglass' Paper, December 1, 1854

The Past is past! with many a hopeful morrow!
  Its errors and its good works live with God:
The agony is o'er of joy or sorrow;
  The flowers lie dead along the path we trod.

The Past is past! in solemn silence taking,
  Alike, the sunny and the rainy day;
On the life altar of the fond heart breaking
  Fall many an idol built on feet of clay.

The Past is past! in certain still rotation,
  Deadening and loosening, as it traveled by,
Each hope that bounds in glad anticipation,
  Each vivid passion and each tender tie!

The Past is past! and our young selves departed
  Upon the flashing whirl of those fleet years;
Its lessons leave us sadder, stronger hearted,
  More slow to live, less prodigal of tears.

The Past is past! and knowledge taught suspicion
  To dim the spirit with its foul, cold shine;
For many a base and dark thing finds admission

---

25 The past is the past, and passed forever!

Amid the wisdom learnt from life and time.

The Past is past! and in that twilight valley
       Dwell slow repentance and the vain regret;
Fears for the future from those shadows sally,
       And hang around the path before us yet.

The Past is past! and ah! how few deplore it,
       Or would re-live their time had they the power;
Though Nature sometimes weakly weepeth o'er it
       At memory of some wrong, or happier hour.

The Past is past! there's bitter joy in knowing
       'T is gone forever; dead and buried deep,
It lies behind, and on life's stream is flowing,
       Where the dark waters of the Dead Sea sleep.

The Past is past! in faith and patience, taking
       Its lessons, let us lay them on our hearts;
The chain's attenuated links are breaking:
       Be earnest!—use the Present ere it parts!

Galileo and the Telescope

How few persons, now when spectacles *and* telescopes *are in such familiar and common use, reflect upon the blessings conferred through the first, or the scientific value of the last. GALILEO improved, if he did not invent, the* lens—*a specimen of which has been recently discovered among ancient ruins in Italy.*

BY LUKE LICHEN [Saratoga Springs, New York]
Frederick Douglass' Paper, June 8, 1855

Perfection of opticians' art,
Beloved at core of human heart,
  As apple of an eye!
Thou givest sight to all purblind,
Thus opening access to the *mind,*
  That else would lack supply.

Of fresh ideas, ever found,
In this wide world, broad-cast around
  The *circle* of man's view;
Beyond which *telescopes* descry
Vast verge of all immensity,
  Existing long, yet new.

For mortals' marvel, as sublime abode,
(In His ubiquity) of GOD,
  To whom true FAITH can see
Through *nature,* by His might reveal'd,
And which had been, from *age,* conceal'd,
  GALILEO! but for thee—

Who, with the *lens,* restored to sight
More than a *prison,*[26] in solar light,
     To NEWTON's ken display'd,
Heaven's hosts, in constellated sky,
Revolving 'round THE DEITY,
     For orbic light and shade.

Ah! when will SCIENCE teach mere man,
With mental vision, how to scan,
     God of the universe! that *place*
Whence centrally THY power sustains,
By *general* PROVIDENCE, which reigns
     Throughout all time and space;

And every *cycle* that shall be
Component of eternity
     For countless worlds above,
And for Galileo's *planet,* too,
Which he restor'd to sages' view,
     And—despite Popes—will *move?* *

*When rising from his knees, and renunciation of heresy, contained in the Copernican system, Galileo is said to have exclaimed, (undoubtedly in a whisper, unheard by surrounding cardinals,) "*E pur si muove,*" which being liberally interpreted means, "The world still moves." How different that devout astronomer, (of course, not mad,) from the renowned Saint who believed his *creed,* because it was impossible!

26 It seems likely that in the poet's manuscript this word was "prism," but when published the word was typeset as "prison."

The Promise of the Past

By ANONYMOUS
The Independent, March 1857

'Tis but of fleeting years a score,
    Since father used to call—
"My son, 'tis time you got to bed;
    Come, say good night to all."
Ah! how unwelcome were the words,
    And how they spoiled the fun!
I wasn't tired, why, not a bit!
    Our game was not half done.

But time has flown, and I'm a man,
    And heavy loads I bear;
For wearily the lagging hours
    Drag on, held back by care!
Too long, too long, are now the days,
    And things are different quite;
How gladly would I now respond
    To father's call each night!

Somehow the thought occurs to me
    That this same rule may hold
When I shall find my race is run,
    And life's bright fires grow cold;
May not the somber messenger,
    Whose call I now would dread,
Come at the last, a welcome friend,
    To bid me to my bed?

The Outcast

By Isabel Hotchkiss [Boston, Massachusetts]
The Independent, December 19, 1858

I asked of the world but a little place,
      A chance to be honest and earn my bread,
I staked my all in the game of life;
      I lost, and have nowhere to lay my head.

'Twas weary climbing the mountain height
      With no one to lend me a helping hand.
I tried, God knows, but I tried and failed,
      My feet sank into the perilous sand.

The play is done. Of the land beyond
      I know so little—my heart is sore;
My brain is reeling—I faint and fall—
      My eyes are dim—there is nothing more.

I know where the river is flowing fast—
      I wonder if I could creep to the brink?
Night tells no tales when the stars are hid;
      My brain is reeling—I cannot think.

No one would miss me, no one would care,
      For I have not a friend on earth to-night.
I tried to be brave, God knows, but now
      Through the deepening shadows I see no light.

I know where the river is flowing fast,
      The water is dark, and cold, and deep,
My brain is reeling—I faint and fall—
      My eyes grow dim—is it death or—sleep!

Life Is Fading

By Terence P.
The Weekly Anglo-African, December 10, 1859

Time is drawing nearer, nearer,
    While our heads are turning gray;
Tears are falling on life's mirror
    Every day!

Time is closing beauty's portals,
    Flowers are blossoming to decay;
Fate is delivering graves for mortals
    Every day!

While our pleasure-beat is rolling
    Over life's eventful spray,
Funeral bells are tolling, tolling
    Every day!

While the laurel wreath is shading
    O'er the fame-lit brow of clay,
Sad we see the garlands fading,
    Every day!

Love, then take your promised treasures,
    Fame is dazzling to betray
Life is fading with its pleasures
    Every day!

Hence, while all things are declaring
       Death a seeker for his prey,
Let us be ourselves, preparing.
            Every day!

Forgotten

By Addie M. Hamilton [Oyster Bay, New York]
The Weekly Anglo-African, December 12, 1863

My love has fled, I cease to grieve,
    For moments passed with thee;
Another now you may deceive,
    And I forgotten be.

My heart's first-love; a woman's pride:
    I centered all on thee;
What pain—another at thy side,
    And smiles for all but me?

Another one may now receive,
    The smiles which once were mine;
Another may thee now believe,
    And worship at thy shrine.

My heart a higher love shall seek,
    Through faith in Him above:
I hear angelic voices speak,
    The whisper "God is Love."

Farm boys mugging for the camera; 1897

It Only Seems the Other Day

By Anonymous
The Union, September 1864

Though swiftly Time, with rapid wings,
  Has borne us from old scenes we knew,
Yet memory oft the picture brings
  In glowing colors back to view;
Thus early friends remember when
  They first as schoolboys met in play,
And yet, though years have passed since then,
  It only seems "the other day."

The form of her we loved of yore,
  To whom we pledged affection's vow,
Will glide before our eyes once more,
  Though but in memory living now;
Of that dark hair one tress alone—
  A treasured gift—is spared decay,
Yet words in that familiar tone
  Seem only breathed "the other day."

The friends appear no more the same,
  That shared our mirth and dried our tears,
Or taught us childhood's favorite game—
  The dear old friends of early years;
But where we ask if they forget
  Those memories of the past, they say—
Though time has wrought some changes, yet
  It only seems "the other day."

A quiet evening at home; 1866

Home

By Xanthos

The Loyal Georgian, January 27, 1866

O! how sweet is the sound of that word to the ear,
    As its joys to our mem'ry does start,
And how soft is the tone of its music to hear
    As it plays on the chords of the heart,
When we're far, far away from the lands of our birth
    And with strangers in strange lands we roam,
We may feel glad and gay with the visions of earth,
    But the heart only thinks, thinks of Home.

O! how charmed is the name, for whate'er is our lot,
    Mid the scene shifting pleasures of life,
Its mem'ry will glow like a sun-brightened spot,
    And illume all earth's cares and its strife.

And when sorrow and sadness steal over our minds,
    Like demons sent forth from the tomb,
Then the heart flits away, till with rapture it finds
    The bright pictures and pleasures of Home.

Like the summer wind's sigh to the forest's young leaf
    Is its music, which steals o'er the soul,
And with fairy-like hand dries the wells of our grief,
    And points *up*, to a far brighter goal.
Then when called from those scenes which we now hold so dear,
    And cease from our wanderings to roam
May we leave all earth's joys and its sorrowful cheer
    And find rest in the "Weary One's Home."

Asking and Giving

By Anonymous
The Missionary Record, July 5, 1873

"Please dear papa," cried our Harry,
    "Get a rocking-horse for me!
One as large as 'Bonnie Bessie'
    That Kriss Kringle gave to Lee!"
And the father, looking downward
    On the eager, upturned face,
Cheeks rose-flushed, and black eyes beaming,
    Thought the pleader full of grace.

Yet he gave no word of answer
    Said him neither yea nor nay;
And the boy, with drooping figure,
    Disappointed, crept away,
Days elapsed, and Hal, forgetting
    Grief in many a merry play
Hears, one morning, papa calling:
    "Harry, boy! Just stop this way."

Harry comes with flying footsteps,
    Stops in wonder and surprise—
Seeing—not a horse on rockers,
    Thing of wood with sightless eyes—
But a real, live Shetland pony,
    Bridle, whip, and saddle too!
Wonderingly, hears papa saying;
    "This, my darling, is for you."

Then a shout, both loud and gleeful,
       Bursts from Harry's rosy lips;
"O papa! How can I thank you?
       May I have his name 'Eclipse'?
Why! I thought you did not hear me
       When you did not say, 'I will,'
And you've given not what I asked for,
       But a thing that's better still."

Thus, I think, our Heavenly Father,
       Seeing, where our faith is blind.
When some good our hearts are craving,
       Seeking long we cannot find,
But withholds the longed-for blessing,
       Leaves our want unsatisfied,
That he may bestow us
       Better gifts than those denied.

Kindness to Animals

By Anonymous
The Concordia Eagle, April 7, 1877

Be kind to the lion and study his will,
  And assist in "inserting the claws,"
And don't interrupt him—keep perfectly still,
  No matter how awkward his paws.

Be kind to the wombat and tapir so mild;
  Be kind to the winsome jackdaw;
Be kind to the tiger, and don't make him wild,
  Or he'll give you too much of his jaw.

Be kind to the oyster, ichneumon, and snail;
  Be kind to the brisk kangaroo;
Be kind to the leopard—and don't tread on his tail,
  Or he'll spot you at once if you do.

Be kind to the gastrapod, gurnard and Rat;
  Be kind to the *matrix torquator*;
Be kind to the *rana palustris,* and cat;
  Be kind to the tuberculator.

Be kind to the bull-fish, the goat and the scape,
  To the yak, whelk, and lesser peewit;
Be kind to the chaste odoriferous ape,
  To the beaver, the perch, and tomtit.

Be kind to the friendly and vigorous flea;
　　Be kind to the bold cockatoo;
Be kind to the pussycat, baalamb, and gee;
　　And be kind to the bow-wow and moo.

Be kind to the phascolome, yarrell, and bok,
　　To the boscovitch, guffin, and skoo;
Be kind to the chuq chug and bold prairie hok,
　　To the wiffin, the smoke, and the spoo.

While the Concordia Eagle *published this poem without author attribution in 1877, the* Clarion of Freedom *published "Kindness to Animals" in 1847 under the authorship of Mrs. E. Coutee, which coincides with the early years of her writing. (This anthology includes two poems—"He's None the Worse for That" and "Forest Prayer"—by Mrs. Coutee.)*

THE CITY OF BALTIMORE, MD. IN 1880. VIEW FROM WASHINGTON MONUMENT LOOKING SOUTH.

A Pleasant Walk at Night

*Our reporter on Monday evening felt so exuberant in consequence
of the balmy breeze and splendid moonlight that he gave us the
following original contribution.*

By Anonymous [Baltimore, Maryland]
The American Citizen, April 19, 1879

Now setting forth upon my course
And going round the city,
Taking reports and making notes,
I was pleased with faces pretty.

Young men, old men and gentlemen,
Were seen this pleasant evening,
While I on getting news was bent,
The world at large seemed pleasing.

The sight at St. Paul Lyceum hall
Brought back those scenes forgotten,
Where youth and beauty resigned supreme,
And mirth and music gotten.

The spelling Bee! That good contest,
Reminded me of school-days
When teacher did caress,
For misspelling the word "always,"

As one by one they left the stand,
I pitied them sincerely,
And wished among the number that

I was standing serenely.

But when I heard the pedagogue
Give words both long and solemn,
A change came o'er this mind of mine,
And I was absent pro tem.

Then, at Douglass Institute,
When mirth and dancing went on,
I sighed alas! should I repine
When amongst this gay throng?

At Samaritan Temple, the Easter Fair,
Was in full bloom beguiling;
Sundry young men, with right smart "tin"
Do come and spend the evening.

Thus I walked on the city o'er,
Till Big Sam sweetly tolled on
The quiet midnight air twelve strokes
And quoth I "I must get home."

The scene will live in future days,
In vivid colors 'fore me,
And I shall e'er remember that
This occurred on Easter Monday.

Sonnet

By Percy Hale
The New York Freeman, August 14, 1886

Was it a dream, those glorious days of yore,
When wrapt within each other's fond embrace
We heeded not the world's insane mad chase
So full our joy we could not ask for more;
How swiftly sped the happy hours away!
How little noted we their winged flight!
The very air was full of purest light,
Where not a cloud of darkness dared to stray!
Unheeded was the past; the future, too,
Forgotten was; the present moments were
Sufficient all to banish every fear,
A perfect calm induce. How much we drew,
In those sweet hours, from all that hope can give,
Such perfect joys I could forever live.

*Miss Harriet Murray of the Sea Island School (South Carolina)
with Elsie and Puss; February 1866*

The Schoolmarm

By H. J. Burdette
The Savannah Weekly Echo, October 15, 1886

See where she comes adown the lane,
    With gladness in her laughing eye,
And in her hand the rattan cane
    Will murder laughter by and bye.

Young love lurks in her merry tone,
    And nestles in her roguish looks,
And long, hard, crooked questions moan
    And sob and sniffle in her books.

Her dimpled hand, that seeks the curl
    Coquetting with her graceful head,
Can make a boy's ears ring and whirl,
    And make the boy wish he were dead.

How much she knows, this blooming rose
    Of human will and human won't;
One wonder is, how much she knows,
    The other is, how much she don't.

Sweet pedagogue, I envy not
    The merry boys who greet thy call;
Thy mother cuffed my ears, good wot,
    When she was young and I was small.

Humidity

By Lewis Howard Latimer [New York, New York]
The New York Age, August 16, 1890

Why do I long to speed away
Where the cooling breezes softly sway
The shading boughs of leafy tree?
Because of the Humidity.

Why do I drink of lemonade
Or foaming beer by Eiceburgh made
Or e'en of cool refreshing tea?
Because of the Humidity.

Why do I buy a palm-leaf fan
And purchase shoes the hue of tan
And go about from waistcoat free?
Because of the Humidity.

Why do I pant in want of breath,
And long e'en for the chill of death
Feeling it must far better be
Than this vile thing—Humidity?

There was a time long years ago,
When of this thing I did not know:
I ne'er had heard nor did I see,
In public print, Humidity.

I wish that I'd ne'er heard of this,
My ignorance was prefect bliss;
What I have gained I cannot see,
In learning of Humidity.

The Ebon Venus

By Lewis Howard Latimer [New York, New York]
The New York Age, September 27, 1890

Let others boast of maidens fair,
Of eyes of blue and golden hair;
My heart like a needle ever true
Turns to the maid of ebon hue.

I love her form of matchless grace,
The dark brown beauty of her face,
Her lips that speak of love's delight,
Her eyes that gleam as stars at night.

O'er marble Venus let them rage
Who set the fashions of the age;
Each to his taste; but as for me,
My Venus shall be ebony.

Visions

By W. H. A. Moore [New York, New York]
The New York Age, July 11, 1891

I dreamt there came a love I ne'er before
Had felt. I cannot tell its shape, it came
As comes the light of morn with just the same
Bright witching spell, and, lo, the dream was o'er.
I dreamt there came a sigh, on wings which bore
It deep into my soul. I felt the shame
Of its drear life, and sought to shift the blame,
When, lo, the dream had fled through dreaming door.
Ah, visions, caught from the light and shadow of
The world's wide fields, I pray thee set the seal
Of thy approving smile upon me here,
That I may learn the weight and worth of love,
That I may taste of pain and have it steal
My hope of selfish joy and griefless tear.

Life

By Lewis Howard Latimer [New York, New York]
The New York Age, February 13, 1892

Life is of seasons spun:
Its warp and woof of night
And day. Its pictured moments
Limned in varying light
And shade; of star and sun,
And blackest darkness, when
The spirit revels in a gloom
Dense e'en to suffocation, with
Myriad phantoms from the womb
Of thought. What then—?
All light? all day?
Or would perpetual black
Hang in the heaven's arch,
Like a pall o'er earth, until the crack
Of doom. I'll have the mingling, if I may;
And on the altar of my heart,
The lamp of hope; to shed its ray,
Brightest 'mid adverse shade,
And pale, when prosperous sun
The pathway clear hath made.

When My Ship Comes Home

By James M. Harrison [Norfolk, Virginia]
The Richmond Planet, May 5, 1894

"When my ship comes home," my mother used to say,
 And I wondered where that ship could be;
That she never came near yet sailing year by year,
 Heavy ladened with riches from o'er the sea.

"When my ship comes home," my neighbors used to say,
 When e'er a little errand for them I ran;
But I was young and gay, I'd skip lightly away
 And be contented with "that's a little man."

"When my ship comes home," I now sometimes say
 While o'er life's trouble I am pouring;
When my ship reaches shore my troubles will be o'er
 I land into eternity, life's mooring.

The Punctuation Points

By Julia M. Colton

National Baptist World, September 7, 1894

Six little marks from school are we;
Very important, all agree,
Filled to the brim with mystery,
      Six little marks from school.

One little mark is round and small.
But where it stands the voice must fall
At the close of a sentence, all
      Place this little mark from school:

One little mark, with gown a-trailing,
Holds up the voice, and, never failing,
Tells you not long to pause when hailing
      This little mark from school:

If out of breath you chance to meet,
Two little dots, both round and neat,
Pause, and these tiny guardsmen greet—
      These little marks from school:

When shorter pauses are your pleasure,
One trails his sword—takes half the measure,
Then speeds you on to seek new treasure;
      This little mark from school:

One little mark, ear-shaped, implies,
"Keep up the voice—await replies!"
To gather information tries;
         This little mark from school:

One little mark, with an exclamation,
Presents itself to your observation,
And leaves the voice at an elevation,
         This little mark from school:

Six little marks! Be sure to heed us;
Carefully study, write and read us;
For you can never cease to need us,
         Six little marks from school!

This poem is a takeoff of "Three Little Maids from School Are We" from the 1885 Gilbert & Sullivan opera The Mikado.

The Man in the Hole

A gentlemen who lives in Iowa has forwarded to us a stirring little poem which he says is founded on fact, and which, moreover, according to his notion, shows that people are too ready to jump at conclusions.

By Anonymous
The Afro-American Advance, July 8, 1899

There was a man in our town
    Who rushed along the street,
When suddenly he felt the world
    Recede beneath his feet.

A teamster had delivered coal
    And then pursued his way—
He left the manhole open, so
    There was the deuce to pay.

The man who hurried never saw
    The yawning hole ahead:
He made some bitter comments as
    He disappeared, 'tis said.

Now comes the moral of the tale:
    A cyclone from the west
Came down the street, as cyclones do,
    And never stopped to rest.

The coal man and his team were first
    Tied into forty knots,
And then distributed in chunks

O'er fifty yards of lots.

The street was ripped from end to end
        And split up through the middle—
Not one who walked in it was left
        To dance or play the fiddle.

But he who hadn't seen the hole,
        And so had fallen through,
Came out, when all was over, just
        About as good as new.

Keep back the things that thou wouldst say
        When Fate seems harsh with thee;
It may turn out the other way,
        So wait awhile and see.

The World's Judgment

By S. F. Kiner
The Afro-American Advance, August 12, 1899

He governs a thousand men,
　　And vast is his worldly store;
Fear enters their hearts whenever he frowns,
　　They gasp when he passes the door.
The bread they eat and their children's bread,
If it pleaseth him to but nod his head,
　　May gladden their mouths no more.

He governs a thousand men,
　　Who tremble beneath his eye;
There is mighty force in his heavy jaw,
　　And his brow is broad and high;
He has only to whisper a word and they
That acknowledge his rule spring forth to obey,
　　Never asking "How" or "Why"?

He governs a thousand men,
　　But his face is puffed and red,
And oft he reels as he moves along,
　　And oft he keeps his bed;
Oft with a gouty foot he has sat,
And oft, instead of his glossy hat,
　　A towel is on his head.

I govern no men; my brow
　　Is neither broad nor high:

But I am master within myself,
      And I yield to no craving cry;
Yet the world knows him and it knows not me,
And so, as the world still judges, he
      Is a greater man than I.

V

Spirit & the Natural World

On the Evening and Morning

By George M. Horton [Chatham County, North Carolina]
Freedom's Journal, August 15, 1828

When evening bids the Sun to rest retire,
Unwearied Ether sets her lamps on fire,
Lit by one torch, each is supplied in turn,
'Till all the candles in the concave burn.

The night hawk now, with his nocturnal tone
Wakes up, and all the owls begin to moan,
Or heave from dreary vales their dismal song,
Whilst in the air the meteors play along.

At length the silver queen begins to rise
And spread her glowing mantle in the skies,
And from the smiling chamber of the east,
Invites the eye to her resplendent feast.

What joy is this unto the rustic swain
Who from the mount surveys the moonlight plain,
Who with the spirit of a dauntless *Pan*,
Controls his fleecy train and leads the van.

Or pensive, muses on the water's side,
Which purling doth thro' green meanders glide
With watchful care he broods his heart away
'Till night is swallowed in the flood of day.

The meteors cease to play, that mov'd so fleet
And spectres from the murky groves retreat,
The prowling wolf withdraws, which howl'd so bold,
And bleating lambs may venture from the fold.

The night-hawk's din deserts the shepherd's ear,
Succeeded by the huntsman's trumpet clear,
O come Diana, start the morning chase
Thou ancient goddess of the hunting race.

Aurora's smiles adorn the mountain's brow,
The peasant hums delighted at his plow,
And lo, the dairy maid salutes her bounteous cow.

On the Sabbath

By W. [Baltimore, Maryland]
Freedom's Journal, September 19, 1828

Hail glorious day, of heavenly birth,
A sacred day to moral worth,
A day which is our God's alone,
A day we cannot call our own.

A day on which we should not say,
Or do what we would every other day—
From worldly bus'ness we should refrain,
And seek for more substantial gain.

A day of rest from worldly care,
And set apart for praise and prayer;
An earnest of eternal rest,
Where all are holy—all are blessed.

A day to preach the Gospel word,
To hear the suffering of our Lord;
A day on which the Saviour rose,
In spite of his malignant foes.

A day on which all christians join
To sing the praise of God divine,
And gives to each a happy greet,
Until in heaven they all shall meet.

Then holy day, we welcome thee,
And from vain thoughts we would be free;
To keep thee right, we'll watch and pray,
And ne'er forget the Sabbath Day.

INTERIOR OF THE CHURCH, FROM THE WESTERN WING.

THE FIRST AFRICAN CHURCH, RICHMOND, VIRGINIA.—[Drawn by W. L. Sheppard.]

1874

Evening

By Mary Gordon
The Rights of All, June 12, 1829

How sweet the pensive hour of even,
      When Nature sinking to repose,
Robed in the loveliest dyes of Heaven,
      Around her glowing shadow throws.

Yon golden cloud, arrayed in beauty,
      So richly tinged with every hue,
What artist's skill can ever portray?
      What pencil e'er so softly drew?

And, see, the lovely star of twilight
      Just glimmering through its fleecy veil,
To hail the rising Queen of midnight,
      Then gently sink behind the dale.

But, where's the charm which sweeps so lightly,
      With thrilling touch each answering nerve;
Does Luna's ray, which beams so lightly
      In robe of light, the spell preserve?

Ah, no! before the star of Vesper
      Had hail'd that silver ray in view,
I felt its power, I heard its whisper,
      Breathed from each cloud of orient hue.

'Tis Nature's all consenting softness
    That sweeps the trembling chords of joy;
'Tis the repose which steals around us,
    When day-light cares no more annoy.

The Snow Storm

By Anonymous
Weekly Advocate, January 21, 1837

Loud the wintry wind is blowing,
Fast descended the gathering snows,
Colder and still colder growing!
Louder still the tempest blows!

Hark! the dreary sounds are clearer,
Spirit of the angry blast!
O! thy shrieking voice is nearer;
Whither dost thou speed so fast?

Woe and desolation bringing,
Com'st thou now to rouse the gale?
Wide thy loosen'd whirlwinds flinging,
Rending every shivering sail!

Hark! o'er land and ocean howling,
Horror marks thy wild career;
Dark, the lowering storm is scowling;
Wild thy sweeping tempests veer!

Now, while dreary winter rages,
While the drifting snows descend,
Who the widow's woe assuages?
Who will be the orphan's friend?

Ye, who bask in ease and fashion,
Rich in all that wealth bestows,
May your hearts, in soft compassion,
Feel a fellow-being's woes.

Mark you the haggard boy's complexion,
See his worn and scant attire,
Give the wretched child protection!
Send his mother food and fire!

God, himself, shall reimburse you,
Swift the widow's prayer shall rise:
Orphan's lips shall never curse you;
You'll have treasure in the skies.

Stanzas

By ELLEN [Fredonia, New York]
The Northern Star and Freeman's Advocate, February 10, 1842

Flowers—which come and pass away,
Too bright, too lovely long to stay,
Deep powers within your beauty lie—
Tell me what it is to die.

Wind so soft, with gentle breath
Scarcely moving the bright leaf;
Strong wind, rushing wildly by—
Tell me what it is to die.

Bird, that mak'st the forest ring,
With thy joyous caroling,
Tarry, ere thou soarest high,
And warble what it is to die.

Ocean, strong and mighty One!
Tell me, with thy mystic tone,
As thou widely sweep'st the shore,
What it is to be no more.

For beneath thy sparkling waves,
Sheltered in thy coral caves,
In a dreamless slumber lie
Those who've felt what 'tis to die.

Nature—thou hast many a tone,
Thou hast language all thine own;
Deep within thee voices lie,
Let them tell what 'tis to die!

Alas! from these there come no breath!
They have no power to speak of Death!
Though they wake within the soul
Feelings strong beyond control.

But thou *something*, hidden word,
Spirit—soul—thy voice I've heard;
And it murmured thus; To die
Is to unveil Eternity!

God Is There

The God of heaven is there—
The earth, the sea, the sky,
All things that are, afar and near,
Tell of his presence nigh.

By J. D.
The North Star, January 21, 1848

The storm that rages, while the billows dash,
The thunder rolling, while the lightnings flash—
The earth that trembles, while the mighty quail,
And fierce volcanoes sulphur fumes exhale—
The dire sirocco on the desert plain,
The whelming iceberg of the polar main;
All nature's elements one language share—
Hear we their voice! "Jehovah, God is there!"

Nor is he only where the thunder roars,
Or blazing Etna's seas of lava pour,
Or stormy billow, rain, and wind, and snow,
Each in its turn is cause of human woe;
His mighty power in these may be discerned,
His wisdom, too, from each and all be learned:
These loudly speak in tones that strike with fear,
And man replies too often with a tear.

The sun uprising in the glowing east,
While dew-drops glisten on each green leaf's breast,
And lovely morning fragrant breath exhales
In verdant meadows and in flowery vales;

The silvery moonbeam sparkling on the wave,
The stars soft twinkling o'er the good man's grave,
The shades of evening gathering o'er the plain,
Far from the scoffing, dissolute, and vain,
The streamlet gurgling, as it softly flows
To the wide ocean, whence its waters rose,
The soft breeze blowing, while the tall trees bend,
And the leaves rustle in the passing wind—
These, nature voices, one language share—
Listen! They speak! "The God of Nature's there."

Nor is he only in the world of sense,
Where reign his wisdom and omnipotence:
Thoughts of the mind—of hope, of joy, of peace,
Sorrow and sadness, happiness, and ease,
Thoughts sweetly welling from the feeling heart,
To rapture swelling, that sense can ne'er impart—
Calm contemplation on the things of time,
Bright expectation of immortal prime,
Sweet meditation on the law divine,
Where truth and wisdom in full beauty shine;—
In these, indeed, we must at once descry;
That God, the God of heaven, is nigh.

Great Deeds

By Elizabeth M. Sargent
The North Star, January 26, 1849

Gently and stilly
    Falleth the dew—
It jars not the lily,
    Hiding from view;
        The lily, from the heavens fed, offereth her prayer,
        And silently the incense riseth on the air!

Slowly and slily
    Openeth the flower;
Watch well and wily,
    From hour to hour—
        Never a tell-tale leaf the mystery discloses,
        The moment when the pale buds open into roses!

Silently and slowly
    Cometh the dawn,
From the skies holy
    Heralding the morn—
        Silently and stealthily go the shades grim,
        And silently goeth up the earth's matin hymn!

Afar in the ether
    Swing the bright stars,
Quiring together—
    No sound the night mars:
Silence keepeth watch in the dark blue halls,

Soundless and echoless her light foot falls!

In the earth dark,
  The small acorn sleeps;
From the cleft bark
  The tender shoot creeps;
Slowly and silently riseth the tree,
And human love is dumb at the deep mystery!

Morning Song

By James Monroe Whitfield [Buffalo, New York]
Frederick Douglass' Paper, July 28, 1854

Awake! 'tis morn,
The brilliant dawn
Has ushered in the day;
The Queen of night
Has paled her light,
The morning star its ray.

Arise, and hark!
The warbling lark
Pours forth its morning lay,
And seems to praise
The sun's bright rays
Which gild the opening day.

Each bud and flower,
From field and bower,
Sheds fragrance all around!
While through the trees
The murmuring breeze
Whispers with gentle sound.

While notes of praise
In varied lays
From all the earth arise,

Pour forth thy song
In notes more strong
And let it reach the skies.

And bear above
Such strains of love
As none but thou canst raise,
Save angel choirs
Who tune their lyres
To sing Jehovah's praise.

Life Is Perfected by Death

By JENNY MARSH [Rochester, New York]
Frederick Douglass' Paper, April 13, 1855

The dead are calm;
No toiling calls them from their rest,
Or lifts their hands so meekly prest;
Upon their brows no fevers burn,
Nor tearful eyes to heaven they turn.
How worn are we!

The dead are blest;
Their hearts have read the mystery,
And rent the veils of futurity,
And now with light around their feet,
They garner knowledge rich and sweet.
How blind are we!

The dead have rest
From all that wearies thee and me,
And oh, how sweet that rest must be!
From yearnings that arouse the soul
To struggles vast, beyond control.
How long, O Lord?

Ye heaven-called dead!
I look at your pillows and have no fear,
The angels will guard, and heaven is near;
The breath of the world plants thorns in my breast,
I long for a pillow whereon I may rest.
Whereon I may rest.

How long, how long?
Ere I shall fall, like a child, asleep,
Unheeding the tears that a few may weep,
With a heart at rest, and a brow all calm,
And a spirit learning the angel psalm?
  Will it be long?

  Bear me, and hear me,
Center of Angels, for I am clay,
And weep and yearn for the brighter day.
Oh, make my faith like a clasping hand,
Leading me on to the better land;
  To the better land.

Untitled

*Charlotte Piles, a noble woman, is now travelling
in the free States, soliciting aid for the redemption
of a part of her family from [. . .] Slavery.*

By Charlotte Piles [Providence, Rhode Island]
Frederick Douglass' Paper, December 14, 1855

Sisters with the heart of Martha,
      Going forth the Lord to meet,
With the love of blessed Mary
      Pouring oil upon His feet;
 Have you heard it? Do you know it?
      Lo! our Lord is in the street.

Loving sisters, ye are many;
      How your heats would throb to know
That along our pleasant city,
      Just released from Slavery's woe,
Hungry, thirsting, faint and needy,
      Christ with weary feet doth go
O, we should not dare to say it!
      But Himself hath told us so.

O, to give our roof for shelter!
      O, to share with Him our bread!
Like the blest Judea woman,
      Bathe His feet, anoint His head!
But He counteth every kindness,
      (We remember He hath said.)
To the least of these His children,

As 'twere done to Him instead.

One of these, His precious members,
      Passeth at your door today,
With the brave heart of a mother,
      Bearing up the shattered clay,
Black and poor, despised and lowly
      For your pity come to pray;
Humbly seeing in her sorrow,
      Sure you will not tell her Nay;
Thus disguised, it is the Master,
      That you lightly send away.

Done to thee, will thou esteem it?
      O, our Savior, done to thee?
When life's burdens grow too heavy,
      This shall our rejoicing be,
Thou hast said it, we believe it,
      "Ye have done it unto me."

Two years after publication of this poem, the Liberator *reported that Charlotte Piles, supported largely by churches and benevolent societies, had raised funds enough to purchase emancipation for her two sons-in-law, whose wives and eight children had previously been manumitted. Charlotte's own son remained in bondage; she had collected more than $600 towards the $1,000-plus demanded for his emancipation.*

No Cross, No Crown

By James M. Smith
Weekly African Magazine, September 1859

If all my path through life should be
      Without a thorn, without a care;
If flowers ever strewed the way,
      If sorrow never entered there;
If all was quiet, tranquil, smooth;
      If happiness reigned without alloy,
If strife and discord never came;
      If all was one continuous joy,

I should be tempted to forget
      The hand that kindly all bestowed—
Forget to thank the God who gave,
      Forget the source from whence it flowed.
I should be tempted to forget
      Myself a sinful worm to be,
That I a moment could not stand,
      Unless sustained, my Lord, by Thee.

'Tis best that sorrow's cloak should fall
      Around us while we're here;
It will but make the joy more great
      When with the Savior we appear.
Let me not grieve if trials come,
      Or if the world upon me frown;
If I have never borne the cross,
      How can I hope to wear the crown?

Thank God for Little Children

By Frances Ellen Watkins
The Weekly Anglo-African, January 28, 1860

Thank God for little children!
    Bright flowers by earth's wayside,
The dancing, joyous life-boats
    Upon life's stormy tide!

Thank God for little children!
    When our skies are cold and gray,
They steal as sunshine in our hearts,
    And steal our cares away.

I almost think the angels
    Who tend life's garden fair,
Drop down the sweet wild blossoms
    That bloom around us here.

It seems a breath of heaven
    Round many a cradle lies,
And every little baby
    Brings a message from the skies.

The humblest home with children
    Is rich in precious gems,
That shame the wealth of monarchs,
    And pale their diadems.

Dear mothers, guard these jewels,
    As sacred offerings meet,
A wealth of household treasures,
    To lay at Jesus' feet.

"Suffer little children . . . to come unto me"; 1899

The Star of the East

By W. S. [Gouldtown, New Jersey]
The Christian Recorder, March 2, 1861

Lo! O'er Persia's plains the sky is lit
By one great meteor, stranger than the rest,
Darting alone its joyful rays to earth.
A new star—one before unknown to men—
Doth from the eastern horizon appear,
Astonishing the sagest of the sage.
Wise men assemble in their fathers' halls,
And search for records of the like event,
But none are found. Then, with sagacious minds,
They search the science of the stars, but find
No theory there to glean a knowledge from.
But higher go the thoughts of wise men;
The great Invisible directs their minds,
And lo! Oh, joy unspeakable!—they lift
Their raptured souls, with grateful thanks, to heaven
"'Tis come, 'tis come," they cry, "God's love is come.
Peace, peace to man now richly is bestowed—
Haste, bring good gifts e'er yet the sun be up,
And then away to worship at the feet
Of Him who in Judea's land is found."
The laden camels now are at the door—
Forth come the wise men with their staves in hand,
And westward ply with gladden'd hearts their way;
And looking to the heavens for signs of day,
The gladd'ning star meets their exultant gaze,
Still looming up from toward the eastern sky,

Rising, till nigh o'er their heads it stands.
On still they go; their hearts, with joyful swells,
Give praise and thanksgiving unto their God.
O'er mountain tops, and in the vale beneath,
Are seen the footsteps of those godly men.
But after days and scenes have pass'd away,
The glorious star still guiding them the while,
They come to Judea's city, Bethlehem,
And lo! behold, the star undimmed doth stand
Above a humble shed, wherein doth feed
The horned oxen when their work is o'er.
In rush the men, can they believe their eyes!
There, seated on its mother's knee, is seen
The Son of God! Glory shines round his head
In one continual, sacred glow of light.
Falling upon their knees, while tears do flow,
With choking sobs, presenting all their gifts
The wise men are. The little child holds forth
Its tiny hand, and with the sweetest smile,
Doth show the gifts are pleasing to God.
Now do the wise men go their way in peace—
Their eyes have seen—their hearts no longer doubt—
And when they reach their vine-wreathed cottage homes,
They meet their kinsmen with one gladd'ning shout
And say, "'Tis come! now we may die with joy."

In this poem the author imagines the birth of the Christ-child from the point of view of the Magi, or "wise men." The Magi, according to the Gospel of Matthew, recognized the birth of the Messiah by the appearance of a new star in the eastern sky.

The Episcopal Mould

By J. Willis Menard [New Orleans, Louisiana]
The Christian Recorder, January 2, 1864

Let him be a man of God,
With religion pure and meek;
Makes no difference if he knows
Neither Latin, Dutch or Greek.

Let him be endow'd of God,
Do not figure out his age;
So he has a judgment firm,
Be he youth or be he sage.

Let him be endow'd of God,
With a quiet and solid mind;—
With a large expansive heart,
That is gentle, true and kind.

Look not at his outward show—
Nor the highness of his name;
Choose him from the high or low,
With a high and holy aim.

One with Wisdom's glowing flame,
Beaming on his mind and heart—
One whose upward steps will ne'er
From the path of *Right* depart.

Sweet Star of Hope

A Sacred Ballad

*The following beautiful lines of poetry are original, and were written
by Miss Angeline R. Demby [...] They have been set to music by Prof.
A. Burris, and will be sung shortly at a Sabbath school Concert, of the
Union Church [...] We have seen quite a number of her compositions,
which we hope will appear in the RECORDER alternately.*

BY ANGELINE R. DEMBY [Philadelphia, Pennsylvania]
The Christian Recorder, January 27, 1866

Sweet star of hope; thou emblem bright,
I see thee oft when sorrow's night
Would o'er my pensive spirit fall,
And teach me on the Lord to call.

Sweet star of hope, I look to thee,
When I would to my Saviour flee,
To lay my sorrows at His feet,
Receiving blessings that are meet.

Sweet star of hope; in midnight's gloom
Thou'lt cheer my pathway to the tomb,
I'll feel that I am doubly blest,
When by Thy rays I find my rest.

Sweet star of hope; in brightness drest,
While leaning on my Saviour's breast,
I'll keep my eyes upturned to Thee;
Thou ever shall my comfort be.

Sweet star of hope; thou guiding star,
That shineth on me from afar,
In ecstacy my voice I'll raise,
To sing my dear Redeemer's praise.

Sweet star of hope; when death's dark vale
Doth cause my beating pulse to fail,
I'll leave thee beaming in the skies,
And shout exulting as I rise.

A Ramble in August

By Anonymous
The Loyal Georgian, August 24, 1867

Come, let us leave the city's din,
    The dry and dusty town,
And wander forth to pastures fresh,
    And meadows newly mown.

We'll gather many a flowering shrub
    Along the old-stone wall,
The speckled lily in the swamp,
    And snowy button ball.

Where interlacing boughs conceal
    The entrance of the wood,
And mystic shadows tempt to trace
    The sylvan solitude.

We'll rest beneath the spreading oak,
    Among its gnarled roots;
The blackberry clambers o'er the rock,
    And proffers us its fruits.

The blackberry clambers o'er the rock,
    And many a flowering wreath
Hangs o'er the alders by the brook
    That darkly glides beneath.

The hardback springs beside the road,
      The fern beside the stream,
Where cool, beneath the rustic bridge,
      The limpid waters gleam.

We'll wander round the ruined mill,
      Far down the quiet vale,
Where many a farm and sheep-cot lane
      Lie scattered o'er the dale.

Till twilight gray the rural scene
      In tranquil beauty blends,
And slowly o'er the eastern hill
      The August moon ascends.

A Summer Morning

By Henrietta
The Christian Recorder, July 30, 1870

In eastern skies a wondrous picture glowed,
Calm azure era's 'mid blooming islands flowed
Where castles, like the storied ones of old,
Stood with their minarets of shining gold.
And ever lightly seemed the waves to play,
On shell-strown shores that peeped through amber spray.

In many a garden waved the silver fir,
The leaves, with dew-drops hung, were all astir;
Wet roses lent the grove aroma rare,
While twittering birds made vocal all the air;
And rainbow cloud flowers op'd their eyes,
To view the gorgeous painting in the skies.

Light stole through mazes where the masses lay,
And shadows fled afar before the day;
The breeze, sweet-scented, carried from the hills
And balmy woods, fed by a thousand rills,
Odors of home; and on the ocean wild,
The mariner thought of his only child.

O peace of early morn! What warbling comes
Borne on the chiming winds and insect hume;
What beauty greets us from the soft-flushed skies,
Bidding our praise, like incense, to arise.
What soothing comes, mild as the dews descend,
To calm our souls and gently with them blend.

Saved at Last

By Frances Ellen Watkins Harper
The Christian Recorder, August 7, 1873

Time with its narrow shores receded,
    And fainter grew life's din;
Behind me lay earth's sorrows,
    Its suffering, want and sin.

Behind me were life's fetters,
    Its conflict and unrest;
Before me were the pearly gates,
    And mansions of the blest.

Behind me were earth's pleasant scenes.
    Its grandeur, gild and glow;
But oh, how faded were the things
    I valued once below,

Honor and fame were fleeting breaths,
    And gold was dust and dross;
The only glory that I saw
    Was streaming round the cross.

Behind me dreadful Incense rose,
    From censers filled with vice;
Before me were the pleasant airs
    That breathed through Paradise.

Behind me were the storms of life,
      Its rocks and shoals were past;
My bark was anchored by the throne,
      And I was saved at last.

Through misty doubts and chilling fears,
      Through storms of wild discord;
The port is gained and I shall be
      Forever with the Lord.

Spring

I herewith send you a poem, written by little George Miller, aged twelve years, and at present a pupil to Howard Colored School, this city [...] In the name of God I present him to the Negro race; and offer myself as one of any sufficient number who will join to insure him a full education. A. A. Whitman

By George Miller [Fort Smith, Arkansas]
The Christian Recorder, April 6, 1882

I stood by a brook
In a shady nook
And watched the waters glide,
I looked on the other side—
The bees are humming!
Hark! Spring is coming!
The waters are leaping,
And I am keeping
Time with the mill
By the side of the hill.

The brook doth glisten,
Now I listen
To catch the sound
Of the hunter's hound,
Far away by the bluff
That is so rough.

The plants are sprouting;
Hear the boys shouting,
And chasing the hare

To his haunted lair!
The birds are singing
All the woods are ringing!
'Mid music so gay
See the squirrel play
And the glad farmer raise
His wheat and his maize!

Oh! happy the mortal who can hear
The voice of his Maker sounding so near!
All proclaim, with prattle or wail,
Thunder crashing! and maddening gale—
All proclaim with one accord
That Jehovah is the Lord!

Near to the End

By R. J. Chiles
The Weekly Defiance, November 11, 1882

Near to the end! how near God knows
  The distance must be short at best,
And few the steps we take before,
  Our hearts that yearn for shall have rest.

We meet to part, the world is full
  Of sad farewells and long goodbyes;
Our lives are transient as the stars,
  That stream across the evening skies.

Near the end! dark seem the years,
  On whose strange, silent floods we go,
And few the breaks in sorrow's clouds,
  Far off but sweetly vague the shore.

Near to the end! oh blessed calm
  Of God's own peace our spirits fill!
Resigned to His wise chastenings,
  We bow submissive to His will.

Take courage Heart, be earnest Life,
  Up from the base lowlands ascend.
To Duty's noble heights, where light
  Falls from thy crown, near to the end.

Why Do I Sing?

By Mrs. L. S. Bedford
The Weekly Defiance, February 24, 1883

Why do I sing? 'Tis hard to tell
Why joyous notes my bosom swell:
Why strains of music, wild and free,
Gush forth in tuneful harmony,
When, underneath a thin disguise,
A sorrowing heart so often lies.

I sing—the siren voice of song
Bears my enchanted soul along
The stream of time to that blest shore
Where mortal cares are felt no more;
And heaven itself were not complete
Without the sound of music sweet.

Why do I smile? Why, mirrored here,
On brows so used to pain and care,
Are gentle smiles that softly chase
Each other o'er a care-worn face?
The heart o'ercast with grief the while—
And yet—'mid unshed tears I smile.

I smile, because to nature true;
Like gleams of sunshine breaking through
The rifted clouds, when storms are past;
Though soft white clouds still overcast
The azure sky, to cheer the scene

Bright rays of sunlight burst between.

Why do I weep? Alas! these tears
Cannot efface the stains of years;
'Tis grace alone can save, I know,
And yet, 'tis well to let them flow;
They soothe the griefs of life's dark hours,
As sunlight smiles through April showers.

And then 'tis written, "Jesus wept,"
Above the grave of one that slept,
While friends and loved ones gathered 'round
With softened tread the new-made mound;
That when thus pressed with grief and cares,
He found a sweet relief in tears.

Transfigured

By R. R. George [Wilberforce, Ohio]
The Christian Recorder, March 22, 1883

Oh, ye that trust our risen Christ,
Was it not death that placed the crown
Upon the work his life had done?
His life, alone, had not sufficed.

Why let our souls be filled with strife?
Why be in bondage to our breath?
What we call dying is not death,
But passing to a higher life.

And Nature gives us type and clew
In all her building; every change
But circles to a higher range;
The old is promise of the new.

The bulb decays, but lo! The shoot
Bursts from its husk, a living thing,
While all the secrets of the spring,
Lie hidden in its clinging root.

A life is greater than its germ;
Think you the moth that flits its way
Thro' all the mazes of the day
Complains it had not stayed a worm?

Murmured the seed of its decay
"I hid beneath the early showers?"
It whispers through a thousand flowers,
Its answers to my heart today.

So one whose life is vexed with cares,
Whose soul is fettered by its clay,
Feels the worn earth-bonds slip away
And stands a spirit unawares.

A Hymn of Praise

Read at the anniversary of the Sabbath schools
of the Philadelphia Conference, May 14, 1883

By T. M. D. WARD
Christian Recorder, May 31, 1883

To Him who spans the azure sky,
    To Him who guides the stars;
To Him we lift our voices high
    Who studs the earth with flowers.

While sunbeams dance upon the stream,
    And rippling brooklets sing,
We come with harp, and voice, and hymn,
    Our praise a tribute bring.

While spring-blooms spangle hill and plain,
    While May buds crown the year,
We come with fuller, nobler strain
    To adore a name most dear.

While Gabriel leads the shining host,
    While Seraphs praise our God,
We come to make His blood our boast,
    Who broke the oppressor's rod.

In regions far beyond the sun,
    Millions of children dwell,
We, too, shall join the white robed throng,
    We, too, the chorus swell.

Press on, ye warriors of the cross,
　　　　Nor from the foeman fly,
Count all on earth but tin and dross,
　　　　And you shall reign on high.

The Temple of Peace

By R. J. Chiles
The New York Globe, June 21, 1884

O sing to me while heaven,
  Is flushed with sunset gold,
And from the rusty harp let strains
  Of sweet, deep music roll;
There's scarcely breeze enough to stir
  The lily's bosom white,
Pour feeling's deepest current forth,
  Sing as you feel to-night.

A star flames on the steeple,
  A silent, radiant fire,
While to the clouds all golden,
  A lone bird mounteth higher;
The sweet-toned bells are pealing,
  Softly the clear notes fly,
All over the silent city,
  Then tremulously die.

I dream of a grand temple,
  Upon its portals white,
Words writ in golden fire,
  Flash out by day and night.
There every wand'rer coming
  Is a most welcome guest,
Kind hands take off his burden,
  And lead him to his rest.

Its doors are ever open,
   There broods perpetual calm,
With holy music flooded,
   Sweet chant and solemn psalm,
And ever and forever,
   The song they sing is this—
"Out of all human suffering,
   Looms everlasting bliss."

Forest Prayer

By Mrs. E. Coutee
The Weekly Defiance, June 29, 1884

At early dawn when birds awake
And into joyous music break,
Before the balmy breath of morn
The echo gives from hunter's horn,
  Then soft and still as is His will
The loving God goes through the wood.

The little brooks his step they hear,
Stop purling in their waters clear,
So that through all the forest air
Naught shall disturb the morning prayer,
  The trees they think, "now let us sink
Our leafy heads before our God."

The wakened flowers bedecked with dew
At once divine His presence, too;
  And quickly from their eyes so bright
Shake off the slumber of the night;
And whisper low, to each, "You know,
  The loving God goes through the wood."

The Cyclone

By Mrs. Helen Lavell
Western Cyclone, May 20, 1886

There's a storm looming up,
      There's a cloud in the sky;
There's an ominous sound
      Which attracts every eye.
With surprise and terror,
      We hear people say;
The CYCLONE is coming,
      Get out of the way.

The cloud is increasing,
      'Tis gathering force
To remove every object
      Impelling its course.
But hark! there's a sound,
      Like the roll of a drum;
Nicodemus is blooming,
      The CYCLONE has come.

It gathers good tiding
      For all of mankind,
And bears them away
      On the wings of the wind;
While abuse, slander,
      Doubt, and dismay
Are caught in the whirlwind
      And scattered away.

Blow on the little tempest,
        Continue to blow;
To all parts of the Nation,
        Let every man know,
In this beautiful land
        There's abundance of room,
Where men of all stations
        May find them a home.

For the old and the young,
        The great and the small,
In this beautiful land
        There are blessings for all,
Which a loving Creator
        With a bountiful hand,
Has scattered them broadcast
        All over the land.

In his goodness and mercy,
        Whether sunshine or showers
Has dotted the hillslopes
        With beautiful flowers.
From the vast rolling prairies,
        The children of toil
May reap a reward
        In the fruits of the soil.

From morning 'til evening,
        The birds gaily sing
'Til the hills with
        Re-echoing melody ring.
All nature rejoicing
        Invites us to come,

And make in this beautiful
        Country a home.

Then blow; little CYCLONE,
        Continue to blow,
In every direction,
        Let every man know,
Though much has been said,
        The half is not told,
There's peace and contentment
        That's better than gold.

The Coming of the King

By W. Carl Bolivar [Philadelphia, Pennsylvania]
The New York Freeman, January 29, 1887

Once through azure gleamed a star,
    Lighting Bethlehem o'er,
Guiding wise men from afar
    To a lowly door
To behold a halo bright,
    Ever more to shine
From the Christ, supernal light,
    Of a God divine.
Alleluia! alleluia! Hearts and voices gladly sing;
Alleluia! alleluia! For the coming of the King,
Echoing over all the earth,
    Down through every age,
Angel hosts proclaim a birth
    And a heritage.
Loudly ring the church's bell,
    Glad your voices raise;
Let the tones of organ swell
    On this day of days.
Alleluia! alleluia! Hearts and voices gladly sing;
Alleluia! alleluia! For the coming of the King.

The Token

By W. H. A. Moore
The New York Age, July 5, 1890

I make for thee a wreath, dear friend,
    Of fragrant dreams, that in the night,
    When sorrow's pain doth spend its plight,
Then softened breath to loss do lend.

The making and the breaking of
    The ties that bind to earth, that give
    To life the worth for which we live,
All suckle at the breast of love.

The dreams of time—the gathered breath
    Of shadows dear, of peace divine,
    Of joy's refrain, of grief's repine—
But feed the loss we find in death.

For men but live and strive for men;
    And living, striving, weave the spell
    Of love and sense of loss that tell
The story of a life, and then

As if to add the passing cloud,
    They bring the memory of a death.
    I know not if on yonder heath
That twittering bird would cry aloud

In grief for loss of mate, and yet
      I've heard no sadder note than bird
      Will utter when some ruthless herd
Of boys have robbed her of her set.

All nature weeps and smiles in turn;
      The great oak stands 'mid Summer's bloom
      A thing of stately joy, in Winter's gloom
He stands there stripped and gaunt and stern.

Against the lead-hued sky forlorn,
      Itself reflecting pain for loss
      Of days of brighter suns, for loss
Of smiles that in the Spring are born.

'Mid Night's Sweet Calm

By W. H. A. MOORE [New York, New York]
The New York Age, October 4, 1890

'Mid night's sweet calm, when day in sleep
Doth feel the breadth and lengthened sweep
Of Time's grim chase to catch the years,
There comes to Earth the chiding fears
      That revel in the starry deep.

Those thuds of woeful pain that steep
The soul in deepest doubts—the tears
Of Faith whose wan sweet face appears
      'Mid night's sweet calm.

'Tis then the soul would madly leap
From Earth, would sadly, blindly weep
The night away. O, light that clears
The shadows, Joy that cleans and cheers
The heart, thou must my soul's peace keep
      'Mid night's sweet calm.

Faith and Hope

By T. M. D. WARD
The Christian Recorder, March 23, 1893

Though seated far beyond the stars,
Where ransomed millions dwell,
Glance upwards thro' the golden bars,
To God thy sorrows tell.

Hear his sweet voice in furtive breeze,
His wrath in thunder peals,
His whisper in the swelling seas,
His smile on fruitful field.

His echoing praises ring thro' space,
From man, angel, bird and flower;
Each hour he gives the needed grace,
Faith's living conquering power.

When heart and flesh and spirit faint
Amid this desert wild,
He listens to each bitter plaint,
Because I am his child.

Though sorrow's bolt my soul hath riven
And wrenched the bleeding heart,
There comes a sense of sin forgiven,
He turns the deadly dart.

Temptation

By Anonymous
National Baptist World, September 14, 1894

Oh, weary yay! so dark, so hard, so rough
    With trials sore beset,
Like those which in that wilderness
    Our Master met.

We struggle on and struggling fall,
    Unless we look above
To Him who sends His messengers
    Of comfort and of love.

We note too much the stones, the thorns,
    Along our road;
Too little note the hands outstretched
    To ease our load.

O living Christ! who hears each moan
    Of sore-tried breast;
Oh, may we know those messengers
    Of love and peace and rest!

To Thee they came when Thou hadst won
    Thy conflict brief.
To us they come in every weary hour
    Of trial or grief.

O angel ministers who strengthen us!
      Forever are ye near,
In all our weary pilgrimage
      Through desert drear.

O angel messengers! stay ever close;
      Give eyes to see.
O Father-heart! give strength to bear,
      And peace in Thee.

Commit Thy Way

By Anonymous
National Baptist World, October 12, 1894

O Lord! I would not take one step alone
Through Life: Thy hand must lead me on;
Sometimes the night is dark, and I would stray
Before the breaking of the day—
          A wanderer lost!

I need a light upon my path to shine!
Thy light, O Lord! may it be mine;
Then may the brightest sun on me go down,
No darkness can upon me frown—
          My feet are safe!

Oft as my journey lay o'er fen and moor,
O'er flood and crag—ways insecure—
Through lonely vale, and gloomy with dismay,
Thy presence did my fears allay—
          Keep near me still!

I know not what my future path may be,
As it has been ordained by Thee;
But rough or smooth, wherever it may lead,
O'er dreary waste or verdant mead,
          Be Thou my guide!

As Thou thus far hast led me on my way
Lead kindly on, O Lord! I pray.

In weakness be my strength; keep firm my feet
Till I the golden city greet—
                    There safe at home!

The Reverend Mrs. J. H. Vigal of Buffalo, New York; circa 1885

In Woodlands

By Unknown
The Afro-American Advance, August 5, 1899

Echoed through the forest reaches,
From the maples, elms and beeches,
    From the dewy dawning to the waning of the day,
Pipes the orchestra of summer
In this shadowland the drummer
    Raincrow beats his bell-toned, deep, elusive lay,
And the purple grackle glistens
As he plumes his wings and listens
    From a pyramidal pine top looming far way,

By the wood brook's mellow margin
Hear the thrush's song enlarge in
    Cadences thrice lifted in delicious, three-fold notes;
And the warbler's call delirious
Mingles with the jay's imperious
    Cry in high branches where the elm's green banner floats,
While a singing marmot pauses
As if seeking what the cause is
    Of this ceaseless chorus from a host of woodland throats.

From the wild grape's vines confining
Comes the catbird's peevish whining,
    And the phoebe's pining in the grasses deep and lush;
While the mourning dove seems ever
Moaning for the lost, and never
    Is a silence but its vague call quavers through the hush.

So loved summer's chorus lingers
In the land of wildwood singers,
  Where the orioles blot the shadows like red poppies in the brush.

Gathering the day's water from a woodland well; circa 1875

Acknowledgments

Voices Beyond Bondage would never have come to fruition without the aid of numerous professionals, friends, and family. While the list of people who have helped us create this anthology is long, we are most grateful to Michael P. DeSimone (M.Ed. CAGS) of Nazareth Academy, Wakefield, for his historical insights and intellectual debates; to Marie E. DeSimone for her unwavering and invaluable support, to Dorothy and William Covolucci for sharing their business acumen, providing us with photoshoot space, and supporting us throughout this entire process; to Billy Covolucci, Matthew Dover, and Vivianne Mello for donating their time and photographic expertise to our project; and to Christopher J. Fortin, David Cope, and Sandy McVetty for providing their insight, knowledge, and assistance as we prepared this manuscript and illustrations for submission to our publisher.

Invaluable research was also provided by: Antony Toussaint and the late Arnaud Beauchamp of the Schomburg Center for Research and Black Culture; Robert Delap of the New-York Historical Society; Thomas Lisanti of the New York Public Library; and Steve Strimer of the David Ruggles Center.

And a special thanks to NewSouth Books for giving us this opportunity.

Image Sources and Credits

JACKET: Front flap, "Family Worship in a plantation in South Carolina," Photographs and Prints Division, Schomburg Center for Research in Black Culture, New York Public Library, Astor, Lenox and Tilden Foundations, n.d. Front cover (clockwise from upper left), "The first vote (*Harper's* Masthead)," Library of Congress Prints and Photographs Division; *Miscellaneous Items in High Demand* collection, reproduction number LC-USZ62-19234, 1867. "Marriage of a colored soldier at Vicksburg by Chaplain Warren of the Freedmen's Bureau," Library of Congress Prints and Photographs Division; *Miscellaneous Items in High Demand* collection, 1866. "A happy family," Library of Congress Prints and Photographs Division, reproduction number LC-USZ62-86365, 1866. "Alphabet of Slavery," Manuscripts, Archives and Rare Books Division, Schomburg Center for Research in Black Culture, The New York Public Library, Astor, Lenox and Tilden Foundations, 1856. *Freedom's Journal* masthead, Vol. 1, no. 10; May 18, 1827; public domain image via Wisconsin Historical Society. "The Statue of 'The Freed Slave' in Memorial Hall," Picture Collection, The New York Public Library, Astor, Lenox and Tilden Foundations, 1876. "Rev. Mrs. J. H. Vigal of Buffalo, N.Y., arm raised, holding Bible," Photographs and Prints Division, Schomburg Center for Research in Black Culture, New York Public Library, Astor, Lenox and Tilden Foundations, 188–. Front cover, center, "Marriage of a colored soldier at Vicksburg by Chaplain Warren of the Freedmen's Bureau," Library of Congress Prints and Photographs Division; *Miscellaneous Items in High Demand* collection, 1866. Back cover (clockwise from upper left), "A political discussion," Library of Congress Prints and Photographs Division; *Miscellaneous Items in High Demand* collection, reproduction number LC-USZ62-127610, 1869. "Gordon as he entered our lines. Gordon under medical inspection. Gordon in his uniform as a U.S. soldier" (Panel I), Library of Congress Prints and Photographs Division; *Miscellaneous Items in High Demand* and *Civil War* Collections, reproduction number LC-USZ62-98515, 1863. "Gordon as he entered our lines. Gordon under medical inspection. Gordon in his uniform as a U.S.

soldier" (Panel II), Library of Congress Prints and Photographs Division; *Miscellaneous Items in High Demand* and *Civil War* collections, reproduction number LC-USZ62-98515, 1863. "Effects of the Fugitive-Slave-Law," Library of Congress Prints and Photographs Division; *American cartoon print filing series*, reproduction number LC-USZC4-4550, 1850. "Jack & Abby," Robert N. Dennis Collection of Stereoscopic Views, Miriam and Ira Wallach Division of Art, Prints and Photographs, The New York Public Library, Astor, Lenox and Tilden Foundations, n.d.. "A slave auction at the south," Library of Congress Prints and Photographs Division; *Miscellaneous Items in High Demand* collection, reproduction number LC-USZ62-2582, 1861. Back flap, "Marriage of a colored soldier at Vicksburg by Chaplain Warren of the Freedmen's Bureau," Library of Congress Prints and Photographs Division; *Miscellaneous Items in High Demand* collection, 1866.

Front Matter: Page xviii (upper left), "Rev'd Samuel Cornish, pastor in the first African Presbyterian Church in the City of New York," General Research & Reference Division, Schomburg Center for Research in Black Culture, The New York Public Library, Astor, Lenox and Tilden Foundations, n.d. Page xviii (upper right), "David Ruggles," image courtesy www.periodyssey.com, scan provided by David Ruggles Center, www.davidrugglescenter.org, n.d. Page xviii (lower right), "Frederick Douglass; head-and-shoulders portrait, facing right," Library of Congress Prints and Photographs Division; *Miscellaneous Items in High Demand* collection, reproduction number LC-USZ62-15887, 1850-1860. Page xviii (lower left), "T. Thomas Fortune," General Research & Reference Division, Schomburg Center for Research in Black Culture, The New York Public Library, Astor, Lenox and Tilden Foundations, 1887.

Section I: Page xxxviii "Alphabet of Slavery," Manuscripts, Archives and Rare Books Division, Schomburg Center for Research in Black Culture, The New York Public Library, Astor, Lenox and Tilden Foundations, 1856. Page 14, "Gordon as he entered our lines. Gordon under medical inspection. Gordon in his uniform as a U.S. soldier" (Panel II), Library of Congress Prints and Photographs Division; *Miscellaneous Items in High Demand* and *Civil War* collections, reproduction number LC-USZ62-98515, 1863. Page 21, "Injured Humanity; Being A Representation of what the unhappy Children of Africa endure from those who call themselves Christians," The New-York Historical Society; call number SY1807, no. 64; negative number 77769d, 1805-08. Page 30, "The Parting–Buy us too," Library of Congress Prints and Photographs; *Miscellaneous Items in High Demand* collection, reproduction number LC-USZC4-2525, 1863. Page 42, "A slave auction at the south," Library of Congress Prints and Photographs Division; *Miscellaneous Items in High Demand* collection, reproduction number LC-USZ62-2582, 1861. Page 50, "Am I not a man and a brother?" Library of Congress Rare Book and Special Collections Division; *Miscellaneous Items in High Demand* and *Cartoon Prints, American* collections, reproduction number LC-USZC4-5321, 1837. Page 70, "The Statue of 'The Freed Slave' in Memorial Hall," Picture Collection, The New York Public Library, Astor, Lenox and Tilden Foundations, 1876.

SECTION II: Page 83, "David Jenkins (1811-1877)," The Ohio Historical Society: The African-American Experience in Ohio, Library of Congress, *American Memory* collection; dbs.ohiohistory.org/africanam/page.cfm?ID=4653, n.d. Page 94, "Effects of the Fugitive-Slave-Law," Library of Congress Prints and Photographs Division; *American cartoon print filing series*, reproduction number LC-USZC4-4550, 1850. Page 98, "Whipping a Negro Girl in North Carolina," General Research Division, The New York Public Library, Astor, Lenox and Tilden Foundations, 1867. Page 114, "Jack & Abby," Robert N. Dennis Collection of Stereoscopic Views, Miriam and Ira Wallach Division of Art, Prints and Photographs, The New York Public Library, Astor, Lenox and Tilden Foundations, n.d. Page 128, "Marriage of a colored soldier at Vicksburg by Chaplain Warren of the Freedmen's Bureau," Library of Congress Prints and Photographs Division; *Miscellaneous Items in High Demand* collection, 1866.

SECTION III: Page 151, "Family Worship in a plantation in South Carolina," Photographs and Prints Division, Schomburg Center for Research in Black Culture, New York Public Library, Astor, Lenox and Tilden Foundations, n.d. Page 162, "Military railroad operations in northern Virginia: men using levers for loosening rails," Library of Congress Prints and Photographs Division; *Civil War* and *Miscellaneous Items in High Demand* collections, reproduction number LC-DIG-ppmsca-10396, 1862 or 1863. Page 164, "A political discussion," Library of Congress Prints and Photographs Division; *Miscellaneous Items in High Demand* collection, reproduction number LC-USZ62-127610, 1869. Page 170, "Gordon as he entered our lines. Gordon under medical inspection. Gordon in his uniform as a U.S. soldier" (Panel I), Library of Congress Prints and Photographs Division; *Miscellaneous Items in High Demand* and *Civil War* Collections, reproduction number LC-USZ62-98515, 1863. Page 182, "Sea-Island School, No. 1 – St. Helena Island. Established April, 1862," Photographs and Prints Division, Schomburg Center for Research in Black Culture, New York Public Library, Astor, Lenox and Tilden Foundations, 1862-69.

SECTION IV: Page 208, "12 African American boys posed at fence," Library of Congress Prints and Photographs Division, *Miscellaneous Items in High Demand* collection, reproduction number LC-USZ62-88082, 1897. Page 210, "A happy family," Library of Congress Prints and Photographs Division, reproduction number LC-USZ62-86365, 1866. Page 216, "The city of Baltimore City, Md. in 1880 View from Washington Monument looking south," Library of Congress Prints and Photographs Division, catalog number 96512994, 1880. Page 220, "Portrait of Sea Island School teacher Miss Harriet W. Murray, with students Elsie and Puss," Photographs and Prints Division, Schomburg Center for Research in Black Culture, New York Public Library, Astor, Lenox and Tilden Foundations, 1866.

SECTION V: Page 240, "The first African church, Richmond, Virginia–Interior of the church, from the western wing," Library of Congress Prints and Photographs Division, *Miscellaneous Items in High Demand* collection, reproduction number LC-USZ62-117891, 1874. Page 259, "African American baby, full-length portrait, wearing christening gown," Library of Congress Prints and Photographs Division, *African American Photographs Assembled for 1900 Paris Exposition* collection, reproduction number LC-USZ62-124653, 1899 or 1900. Page 293, "Rev. Mrs. J. H. Vigal of Buffalo, N.Y., arm raised, holding Bible," Photographs and Prints Division, Schomburg Center for Research in Black Culture, New York Public Library, Astor, Lenox and Tilden Foundations, 188-. Page 295, "Coming from the well. Worsloe, the DeRenne Plantation, Isle of Hope," Robert N. Dennis Collection of Stereoscopic Views, Miriam and Ira D. Wallach Division of Art, Prints, and Photographs, New York Public Library, Astor, Lenox and Tilden Foundations, 187-.

Index of Poem Titles

Index of First Lines